Gone the Way of the Earth:

Indian Slave Trade

in the Old Southwest

Gone the Way of the Earth:

Indian Slave Trade
in the Old Southwest

Clifford J. Walker

Mojave River Valley Museum Association

Barstow, California

Author Clifford J. Walker (1930-   )

First Edition: 1965, Written by Gerald A. Smith and Clifford J. Walker and originally published by the San Bernardino County Museum Association.

Second Edition: 2005, Mojave River Valley Museum Association

Third Edition: 2009, **Mojave River Valley Museum Association,** with funds furnished by the Bill "Shortfuse" Mann Publication Fund. Publication Committee: Clifford Walker, Steve Smith, Pat Schoffstall

Library of Congress #

ISBN: 0-918614-33-3

First Printing 2009

1. Indian Slave Trade in New Mexico, California, Utah and Nevada. 2. Indian Slave Trade in the Southwest. 3. Peonage System in New Mexico. 4. Treatment of Indians in California—1769-1865. 5. Old Spanish Trail—1829-1848. 6. Mormons and Indian Relationships. 7. Indian Slavery in the West 8. Missions--California and Indians

Cover photo: *The Mohave* by Edward Curtis (1868-1952) from *The North American Indian,* Vol. 2, p. 48. This haunting photograph, taken probably after 1900, symbolizes the fine physical features of the Mojave people. He is overlooking the Colorado River toward the sunset in the west, home of generations of Mojave for several thousand years.

Back cover: Background photo by Walter Fuller of *Avikwame,* Spirit Mountain, sacred to Mojave Indians, home of souls of departed Mojaves.

Cover, book design and digital preparation by Dick Tristao's TwoBitGrafix. Visalia, California.

A Mojave River Valley Museum Association Publication
P.O. Box 1282
270 E. Virginia Way
Barstow, California 92311
760-256-5452
mrvm@verizon.net

DEDICATION

To all those victims of Indian slavery in the Southwest whose

thousands of stories will never be told—

They lost their lands,

their songs, their lives and their freedom—

All gone the way of the earth.

To them, we dedicate this book.

TABLE OF CONTENTS

List of Maps

"Wickiups in encampment. Kaibab Plateau," by John K. Hillers, Powell Expedition, 1871-1875. Smithsonian Institution National Anthropological Archives, Neg No. 1633. Typical Paiute shelter found all over the Great Basin.

Paiute Girls "Antinaints, Pu-tu-siv and Wi-chuts in native dress," from the Vegas in Southwestern Nevada by John K. Hillers, Powell Expedition, 1871-1875. Courtesy of Smithsonian Institution National Anthropological Archives, Neg No. 1648-A. Notice the basket hats the girls wore. Young teenager Indians like this sometimes sold for up to $300 in New Mexico.

Acknowledgments

Thanks to Patricia Schoffstall who put the original copy on the computer and did serious editing, to David Dillon who helped with formatting the drafts, and to Mary Shearer and Kathy Kellar for their map making skills. Thanks also for the help of the New Mexican State Archives, The Huntington Library, California State Library, New Mexican State Historian Estevan Rael-Galvez for help in New Mexico, Patricia Kuhlhoff for encouragement and editing in New Mexico, Dolores Kassiones for help in researching and editing, Jane Kolar, Ira Gwin and Nancy Smith for editing, and Grace Nicklaus for editing the Spanish. Thanks to Marjorie Mefferd for helping research, and to June Zeitelhack and Kathy Kellar for original art. I appreciate the good eyes of photographers David Dillon, David Romero and Walter Feller. For computer help, I appreciate Computer Consultant Linda DeWald.

As an historian I have the utmost respect for those who conscientiously dug deep to find historical truth that was available for me and others to use: Elizabeth Warren, the prolific husband and wife teams of Leroy and Ann Hafen and George and Helen Beattie, James Brooks, Joseph Sanchez, Leo Lyman, Dale Morgan and many other great historians.

For my researching years ago, I can't forget the cooperation of the Bancroft Library in Berkeley, Los Angeles County Museum and San Bernardino County Museum, and William Mason of the L.A. County Museum for translating Spanish documents.

I appreciate the Mojave River Valley Museum that encouraged me to expand the Indian slave trade story, the Old Spanish Trail Association and the Mojave River Valley Museum for their work in preserving our heritage for future generations.

Falling in love with the desert, the people, sunrises, sunsets, pinks in the mountains, shadows constantly changing the vistas, and the creosote smells when it begins to rain—these are the reasons I came to the desert to teach for one year in 1955 and never left. These are the reasons I wanted to learn the heritage of this great land.

I must remember my wife Barbara Busch Walker of 56 years who allowed me time and freedom to pursue my love of history and research of the Mojave Desert and California. She patiently typed draft copies over and over. To my children, grand children and great grand children who give me joy and make me realize how blessed I am—thank you all.

Despite help with researching and editing, all errors are my responsibility. Please let me know of any errors so they may be corrected in the next printing.

Clifford J. Walker
Mojave River Valley Museum Association
2009

Preface

In 1776 Padre Francisco Garcés traveled up the Colorado River, across the Mojave Indian Trail to southern California, then north into the San Joaquin Valley, back to the Mojave Trail again, and east to the Hopi village of Oraibi. In the same year the padres Escalante and Dominguez journeyed north from New Mexico into Utah, into the Great Basin, and back to New Mexico. These two treks spurred on the dream of uniting the two far-flung Spanish provinces and their capitals: Santa Fe, New Mexico, and Monterey, Alta California. The lofty dreams of Spanish officials in Mexican City and the northern frontiers of New Spain in the 1770s were left on the desert floor because of the Massacre of Yuma in 1781 and because Spain was close to bankruptcy, facing pressing problems in Europe. A few years later Spain tried to keep her American colonies from ceding from the Spanish Empire.

But Escalante and Dominguez inadvertently helped expand the Ute-New Mexican slave trade that had been going on for 175 years or so. New Mexicans found products in the Great Basin to buy: Indian slaves, the Paiute, Shoshone, Goshute and non-horse riding Ute Indians. Utes who developed a horse culture became more like the Plains Indians. They captured or bought defenseless Indian women and children to sell in the New Mexican markets or to New Mexicans who traded in the Ute territory. From 1776 on slave trade flourished in northern New Mexico and in what is now Utah.

It was 50 years later in 1826 when American trapper Jedediah Smith crossed into the Mojave Desert on the Mojave Indian Trail. New Mexican businessman Antonio Armijo initiated what became the Old Spanish Trail in 1829-30 which ran from New Mexico to California over a 1,200 mile circuitous and arduous route. Their New Mexican successors fulfilled the dream of the Spanish in the 1770s when they opened this trade road to California.

California profited by selling hundreds of excess horses and coveted hardy California mules; conversely, New Mexicans found a market for their fine New Mexican and Pueblo Indian woolen products.

Where the Old Spanish Trail went through Paiute territory from New Mexico, traders captured relatively defenseless desert Indians and sold them in California. On the return trip, they also took Indians captives and sold them in New Mexico.

The Old Spanish Trail tied the two provinces of the Republic of Mexico with Indian slavery. Slavery permeated the whole territory and lasted even after Americans took over the Southwest.

Indian culture was often brutal, depending on tribal customs and their neighbors. Most tribes had some sort of ritual warfare, revenge, capturing prisoners, torturing them sometimes, trading them, and often accepting women and children as adoptive members of the tribe.

Then Euro-Americans (French, English, Spanish and later Americans) came looking for furs and hides. Indians exchanged furs for mirrors, metal pots, knives and hatchets, fire-starting devices, and--very decisively--guns and horses. These items changed the values of the tribes. For example, instead of Native Americans killing their brother the deer just for food and clothing, they killed animals for furs to trade. They often had aggressive fights over lucrative hunting areas. Across the country these forces changed the values of the Native Americans, who then "needed" metal conveniences, guns and horses. When the Comanche obtained slaves, they were immediately set them to work tanning or scraping hides. When hides were more difficult to obtain, slaves became a commodity to sell, especially to New Mexicans.

With Europeans also came their attitudes of superiority, with various "Christian" and "western" values toward land ownership, work ethics, soul saving, social behavior, greediness, revenge and subjugation. And as this book will explain, sometimes came genocide, removal, and slavery.

No matter how ruthless Native Americans had been or Europeans were, they had much in common: falling in love and bonding customs, raising their children to become adult men and women, taking care of their elderly, disposing of their dead, teaching values of the tribe (and families), and explaining the world around them and their role in that world—these are the universal experiences of man.

Man obtains his identity in various ways: his family, neighbors, songs and stories that explain the past and the world, his art, language, and land from which he derives his sustenance, clothing and housing. The Paiute world creator Sinop, for example, gave the Southern Paiutes their land in the Great Basin and he also gave the obligation to take care of that land.

When a young Indian girl was taken into captivity and sold into slavery, her elements of identity were destroyed: her land was taken from her—gone! So too were her language, songs, relatives, stories, customs and perhaps a part of her soul. A part of her was destroyed forever. A part of her was "gone the way of the earth."

This is the slave trade story in the Old Southwest, on the trails, in missions, in former isolated rancherias, and with the victims of a raid. Thousands of lives, songs and dreams unfulfilled have "gone the way of the earth."

Introduction

The Indian path, the mule trail of the Old Spanish Trail caravans and the wagon ruts of the 49er road—all traces of the past-- are found in the Southwest, all evidence of those who came before, all scars left by travelers who lived, breathed, dreamed, and survived until their time came to leave, until they had "gone the way of the earth." These people left only occasionally scars, and their untold stories disappeared. Scarce artifacts were recovered along these tracks; few diaries were written or passed on to become a record of the heroic struggle to survive and fulfill their dreams.

We just don't know who they all were, where they were going or coming home from, the good or bad things they did. A spear point can't tell us the language they spoke, the songs they sang, their dreams that died.

We have some clues: diaries, artifacts, sales memos, articles or letters they wrote or newspaper accounts; unfortunately, only scraps of words passed on to the present generation. Historians and anthropologists try to piece some fragments together and imagine what happened in the past. The infinitesimal minutiae that remain are but grains of sand in the vast desert.

But that's all we have to work with. *Gone the Way of the Earth* is certainly an inadequate book but tries to capture a little, very little, of the Indian slave activity in the Southwest. Slavers were not forthcoming with outsiders; they didn't relate their gruesome adventures to the press or historians. The victims had even less opportunity, or perhaps inclination, to narrate their tragic experiences.

The rest is left to our imagination. Our humanness, perhaps our emotions and our empathy, can help us imagine what slave victims and slave perpetrators experienced. Let your imagination fill in some pieces of what happened in thousands of incidents of this horrid past.

Right: Two Paiute boys, courtesy of Smithsonian Institution National Anthropological Archives, SPC 001879.00 "Pahutes." Although these boys were photographed after Indian slavery stopped, they are typical of the Paiute youngsters who were stolen from their parents and sold to New Mexicans for slaves, domestics or peons.

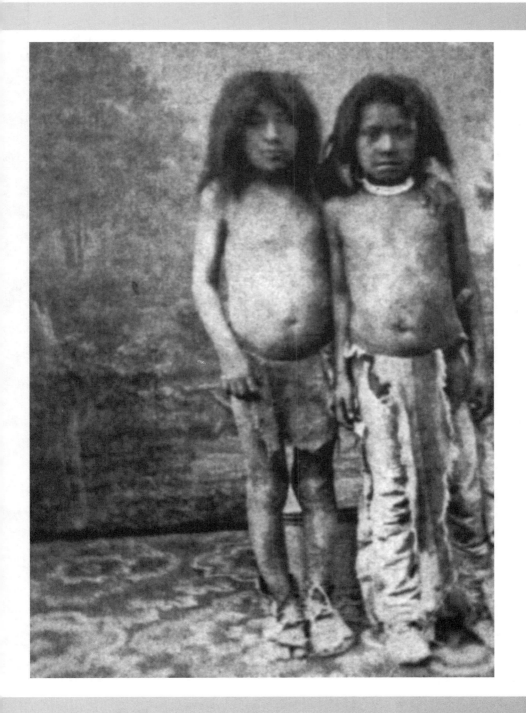

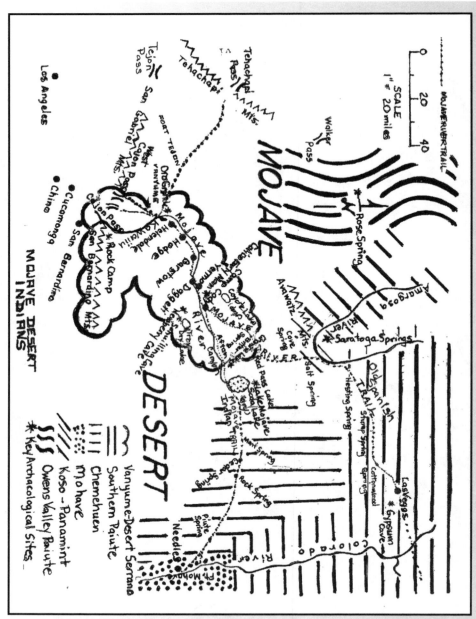

Mojave Desert Map, drawn by William Walker, showing some variant routes. On the west there are various passes that lead to the main water source—the Mojave River— Walker pass, Tehachapi Pass, Tejon Pass, West East Cajon Passes. On the east side of the Mojave Desert, the trails go to Las Vegas, directly to the Colorado River or southeast to the Needles area on the Colorado River. The names vary as well: Mojave River Trail, Mojave Road, Old Spanish Trail, Mormon Road, Los Angeles-Salt Lake Wagon Road, 49er Road, Southern Route, Mojave Indian Trail.

Drawn by William Walker and Kathy Kellar.

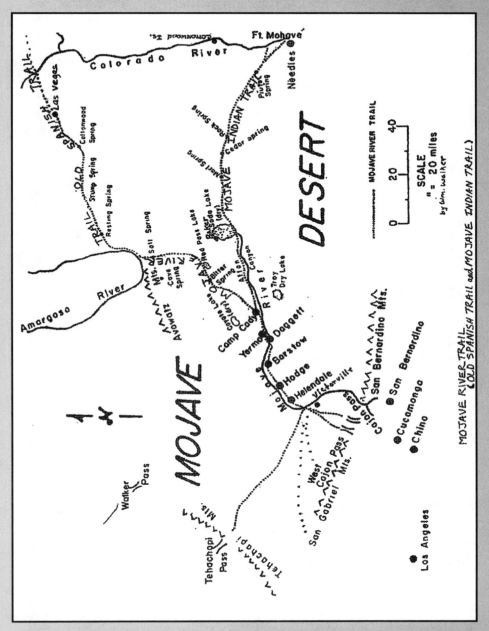

Mojave River Trail, from water hole to water hole across the Mojave Desert—sometimes used for horse thieving, Indian raids and Indian slave trading. Map drawn by William Walker.

House rings or circles or sleeping circles, left over from Paiute encampment in the central Mojave Desert. These camp areas were remains of wickiups where Paiutes once lived. Here may have lived some Paiutes who were taken from the Mojave Desert and sold as slaves in either New Mexico or California by New Mexicans on the Old Spanish Trail, 1829-1848.

Photo by David Dillon

Original sketch by June Zeitelhack

The Southwest and Indian Slavery

It was cold that afternoon in November in 1839 as the New Mexican muleteers efficiently broke down the mules, unpacking them, and with the help of the servants creating shade from the late afternoon sun and windbreaks for the night camp. While the muleteers lazily watered their mules on the southern curve of the Amargosa River, servants prepared atole and piñole and beef jerky for the dueños or business owners of this annual New Mexican trading caravan to California.

Three serape-wrapped Mexicans left the caravan camp and headed down the Amargosa. They raced their horses the five miles from the camp on the river to tiny Amargosa Spring and Salt Creek nearby. As their animals tired, the men slowed their pace to sneak into little Amargosa Canyon. Two rode up the sandy wash to Amargosa Springs. The other rode around the hill, but there were no Indians this time at the springs. Then the horsemen joined at the top of the canyon and headed over the mound that divided Amargosa Spring from Salt Creek. On the west side of brushy Salt Creek they spied a small encampment of Indians. The New Mexicans charged down the hill and through the dusty alkali sand of the ancient Ice Age lake bed and surprised a slim girl filling an olla with water, catching her before she could run. A young man and an older woman ran up the creek, dodging between the arrowweed bushes, cane and tules. The man on the mule didn't care about the male Indian running away, but he searched for almost an hour for the woman without finding her.

The other two men had the girl's hands tied and her leg tethered to a huge arrowweed bush. Her head down, her black hair covering her face, she was sobbing uncontrollably, gasping for air. She was about 10 years old, perhaps measuring 4 feet, 10 inches, skinny and looking undernourished, and wore a short overlapping reed skirt tied around her waist.

These three men would share the extra profit derived from selling this young girl to the Californios. To make her more marketable, they would feed her corn cakes, piñole and jerky to put a little weight on this waif of a girl before they arrived in Los Angeles.

Back at the camp they turned her over to the servant of one of the Mexicans. She was in his hands; she would eat to gain weight, learn to obey and repeat her first Spanish words. Her mind, however, would be filled with fearful thoughts and longing and sadness for her small family. She would notice the landmarks of her home disappearing as the caravan headed steadily toward the southwest. First the Salt Hills, then Kingston Peak, and in a few days the Avawatz Mountains—special homeland places will disappear and her desert home would be gone and her family would only be sad memories as she was taken to be sold to the Californios.

This one composite incident is not unlike hundreds that occurred in northern New Mexico, southern Utah, and after 1829 along the Old Spanish Trail which went across the Mojave Desert to southern California. It is an example of the horrors that happened to isolated Paiute families or extended families that had the misfortune to be in the way of the horse-riding Utes who for years raided Paiute camps in southern Utah for slaves to sell in New Mexico. After 1829 both Utes and New Mexicans raided unprotected Paiutes to obtain women and children to sell to traders on the Old Spanish Trail between New Mexico and California or to sell directly to the Californios or to the New Mexicans.

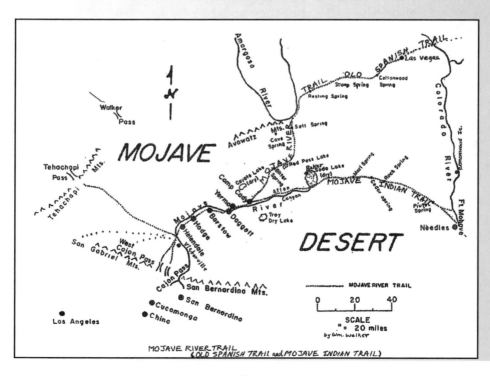

MOJAVE RIVER TRAIL
(OLD SPANISH TRAIL and MOJAVE INDIAN TRAIL)

The institution of slavery has had wide distribution in time and geography and technique. It has existed throughout the world, involving all races over a period of many thousands of years. This inhumane yet human institution existed in North America before the coming of the Spanish-speaking people in the sixteenth century.

The American Southwest had a history of slavery (and some unique features of human bondage) during the Indian, Spanish, Mexican, and American periods. An important area and link in the slave trading in the Southwest was the Mojave Desert's ancient Mojave Indian Trail, a route that actually stretched beyond the confines of the Mojave Desert itself. It went from east of the Colorado River to the Mojave River and across

The Name "Mojave River Trail"

The ancient trail across the Mojave Desert has been used for over 4000 years, namely centering on the Mojave River that runs (sometimes underground) across half the dry Mojave Desert. Desert water holes on both ends of the Mojave River make water accessible to travelers for 360 miles across the relatively dry desert. From the Virgin River in southern Utah to Los Angeles, there are 15 desert water holes, counting the Mojave River as one. These water holes were essential for safe travel across the desert. Native Americans lived at all these water holes--at least seasonably--and have been traveling and trading through the desert for over 4,000 years. Each Indian group had names for the sites. The trails across the desert have had various names over the years. One main route, basically from the Colorado River to San Gabriel, was called Mojave Indian Trail. It is also known as the Mojave River Trail (Walker), the Mojave Road (Casebier), the Old Government Road (after 1858). The road from Las Vegas to Los Angeles has been called the Old Spanish Trail (wrongly named because it is neither "Old" nor "Spanish" as it was started by Mexicans under the Republic of Mexico in 1829-30 as a caravan pack mule trading route to California; the 49er Road; Mormon Road; the Southern Route (Lyman); and the Los Angeles-Salt Lake Wagon Road (by surveyors in1854). Now we have I-15 and partly I-40, going to Las Vegas and Needles respectively. Punta del Agua or Forks in the Road has been moved from Minneola Road east of Yermo and Daggett to the center of Barstow where I-15 and I-40 separate heading east.

the San Bernardino Mountains to the Pacific Ocean. Another trail made a circuitous route from Las Vegas to the Amargosa River, Bitter Springs and the Mojave Desert. The various routes across the Mojave Desert basically went from water hole to water hole to the major source of water, the Mojave River.

Humans have a propensity to covet what other groups have--hunting grounds, fishing spots, fertile soil, trading items, piñon trees, obsidian quarries. Whatever is of value other people want. Another tendency seems to be that stronger tribes or communities pick on weaker ones. Since conflicts occur between units of people, animosities and alliances develop. Attacks, ambushes, thefts occurred throughout the Southwest between Indian tribes, and so did counter attacks for revenge for previous wrongs which sometimes continued for years. Taking captives became a part of the culture as these prisoners were treated in sundry ways depending on their age or sex: they might be killed, tortured, raped, adopted to add to tribal population, married or used as slaves.

Despite Queen Isabella's direction to treat Indians with respect and humanity and as a free people, Spain allowed Indians to be used for labor, supposedly free, consensual labor; but in reality, circumstances, attitudes and greed enabled Spanish officials to ignore the intent of the Queen's laws and exploit Indians of the New World. Two hundred years of Spanish vacillating policies allowed Indians to be enslaved, punished for misbehavior, enslaved as prisoners of war or assigned as contractual labor, supposedly willingly [see Appendix C].

Conversely, Spanish law allowed that if natives didn't yield the land, they must be "slain or taken as prisoners of war and be branded and pass as slaves." The Spanish had the attitude that God sent them as settlers to help "teach them (Indians) good customs."

Officials treated labor as taxes; native work was an obligation (*tributo*) to the *encomenderos,* that is, the owners who were granted the care of the Indians that came with the lands they were granted, or granted to the silver miner who received a contract for so many Indian laborers. This *encomiendera* policy benefited the white man or *mestizo* to the detriment of the Indian. Natives were often duped by those who knew the law, the language and the loopholes. An Indian, for example, might volunteer to labor for the *encomendero* of his village, but if he did not fulfill his obligation or ran away, he could be punished or sentenced to forced labor. He could even be sold. He was a slave.[1]

Juan de Oñate in 1598 took possession of what is now New Mexico and demonstrated his ruthlessness as a Spanish colonizer. He promised the Pueblo Indians peace, justice and prosperity; and he vowed that if they converted to Catholicism, they would have everlasting bliss instead cruel torment.

When Acoma Pueblo resisted Oñate, a fierce fight ensued. After three days of fighting that killed 500 men and 300 women and children, the Acoma offered corn meal, blankets and turkeys for peace. The Spanish refused, and the Acoma received torment in Oñate's revenge. He put many warriors in a kiva, executed them one at time, and threw their bodies off the cliffs. After a trial at Santo Domingo Pueblo, the Spaniards cut off the right foot of male survivors over 25 and sentenced them to 25 years of servitude. Officials condemned the12 to 25-year-old males to 25 years of slavery. Two unfortunate Hopis were at Acoma at the time of the Spanish attacks. Spaniards cut off their right hands and sent them back to the Hopis as a warning. Oñate sent children to the care of Franciscan priests so they "could attain the knowledge of God and the salvation of their souls." Officers escorted 60 to 70 young women to the Viceroy in Mexico City, where they would serve as slaves for 25 years.[2] Oñate portended what was to come in the American Southwest.

Slavery, however, was not introduced by the Spanish. Many Indians already had slavery as part of their war customs. Comanche, Kiowa, Apache, Pawnee, Pueblo had been seizing captives before the advent of the Europeans.

Slavery of various types existed from coast to coast before Europeans came to North America. Debra L. Martin in "Ripped Flesh and Torn Souls: Skeletal Evidence for Captivity and Slavery from the La Plata Valley, New Mexico, AD 1100-1300," pointed out that prehistoric Pueblo villages had active slavery. Skeletal remains of over 20 percent of women in La Plata, Arizona, showed multiple traumas to the head or bodies that healed over and were damaged again. These were compared to male skeletons, children, and females who were buried with possessions of beads or pottery. It appeared that most of these abused or wounded women were of a lowly status, hence slaves or captives. Some were haphazardly dumped in graves, rather than with knees flexed, and most had no grave offerings.[3]

"Wu-nav-aii, gathering seed"—a Paiute woman in 1873 by John K. Hillers, Powell Expedition, 1871-1875. Courtesy of Smithsonian Institution National Anthropological Archives, Neg No. 1641 (Hillers Catalogue No. 53) Notice the two baskets, the large one on the ground is used to catch the seeds hit off the desert plants. The Numic branch of the Uto-Aztecan language speakers harvested the desert seeds and survived 5,000 years in the desert.

One woman had a severe cranial wound on the left side. She healed but was so severely damaged that her right side had been under-developed, atrophied with small right arm and leg, like a stroke victim. She probably lived the rest of her life as a slave, a left-handed slave.

Other examples of slavery are found within the Hurons and Iroquois in the east and with Indians of Northwest coast of the United States. Iroquois raiders, for example, went as far as Michigan to take captives. Cherokees had slaves. Oregon and Washington's Cayuse, Chinook and Walla Walla Indians were all deep into slave catching and trading. Northwest California had Indians, especially Yurok, who acquired wealth for prestige, and slaves became part of their value system. In Grasshopper Pueblo in north central Arizona slave catching was evident as well as among Apache, Comanche, Navajo, and among the Plains Indians.[4]

After European contact with Indians, Utes migrating from Utah into Colorado obtained horses from the Spanish in the 1600s, 30 years before other mountain or plains people became horse riders. They traded prized soft white buckskin for Spanish knives, kettles, axes, wool products and horses. They found their Ute slaves more valuable than finely-made buckskin. As a result these mobile Utes raided Pawnees in Kansas, capturing women to sell to the Spanish for more horses. Jicarilla Apaches, adopting a Pueblo-type culture, later evolved into a horse culture on the Arkansas River and raided Pawnees and tribes in Oklahoma for slaves, again trading them to the Spanish for more horses.[5] In fact, a couple tribes used the word "Pawnee" as synonymous for word "slave." But Pawnees also captured slaves and had ritual killings of captive women.

Comanches left their Shoshone brothers in the Rocky Mountains and received guns from the French trappers on the Missouri River. They pushed other tribes as they moved south, closer to the source of Spanish horses These aggressive people with guns forced the Jicarilla Apache out of Colorado. Even with Spanish as allies, these Apaches could not withstand the Comanches. All these people at various times fought each other, yet traded together for slaves and sold them to the Spanish. Utes and Navajos warred and both sold captives to the Spanish. Over the years Utes even pushed Navajos out of Colorado.[6]

Unfortunate people lived near more powerful and aggressive neighbors. Pit River Indians in northern California, for example, had the misfortune to live near the Modocs and the Klamath Indians and suffered countless raids on their villages as a result. The most unfortunate were the Numic and Takic branches of the Uto-Aztecan speakers who lived in the Great Basin, southern and eastern California, Nevada, Utah, and parts of Oregon, Idaho, Wyoming and Colorado.

Linguistic evidence indicates Uto-Aztecan ancestors migrated from northern Mexico to the Tehachapi-Antelope Valley area of the Mojave Desert about 5,000 years ago. They survived by efficiently using the desert and mountain resources even though the desert became drier after the end of the Ice Age.

Not only did they survive for 250 generations, but the Numic branch expanded to become Shoshone, Paiutes, Ute, Chemehuevi. They spread into the Sierra Nevada, northeastern California, southern Oregon, Idaho, Wyoming, part of Colorado, all of Utah, and most of Nevada except where the Washoe were located. The Takic branch expanded to include the western Mojave Desert (most of the Mojave River), San Ga-

"The Ra-vo-koki or Circle Dance" Paiute in winter wear of rabbit skin blankets on the Kaibab Plateau, by John K. Hillers, Powell Expedition, 1871-1875. Courtesy of Smithsonian Institution National Anthropological Archives, Neg No. 1623.

briel Mountains, San Bernardino Mountains, and southern California to the San Diego County line.

As anthropologist Allan Lonnberg pointed out, there is a difference between appearance and reality. These successful Numic and Takic branches of the Uto-Aztecans appeared different than they really were. The Spanish, Mexicans, Americans and indeed other Indians often looked at these people with a jaundiced eye.   As remarkable as these Native Americans were to survive and expand, perceptions of some of them were most unfavorable. Actually two tribes of Numic speakers became aggressive predators; most of the others became victims of slavery.

Ute and some Shoshone Indians who acquired the horse and adopted some Great Plains culture had respect of the Spanish. Hopis had earned it, especially because of their stubbornness, as had most Pueblo people.   Comanche members went to the southern plains terrorizing Indians, Spaniards in New Mexico and Texas and later Mexicans. Their tribe increased tremendously because of their captives, thus garnering respect. Perhaps *fear* might be a more accurate term than *respect*. These Indians fit more the ideal perception of what noble Indians should be like: Iroquois, Cherokee, Creek or Lakota.

But survivors who conquered the hard life in the desert remained in the deserts and the Great Basin and were maligned by the Spanish and other Indians.   They did not adopt the horse culture—except as huge protein feasts. They lived on small animals, rodents and billions of processed seeds; they "harvested" the deserts and the mountains to sustain year-around life. One Chemehuevis Indian said that to the white man the desert is a wasteland; to the Chemehuevi it is a supermarket.[7]

Despite their remarkable success living in a generally hostile environment, these nomadic desert families developed a negative reputation, an unfair perception by Mexicans and later by Americans. These were the pedestrian Numic and Takic speakers, hunters and gatherers of the Great Basin, eastern California; and to some extent these Indians were lumped together with California Indians and often called "Paiute."[8] But worse, travelers and settlers often classified California Indians with the derogatory term "Diggers." The same is true with the Goshute, Western Shoshone, Shivit, and some non-horse-riding Ute Indians in Utah—who too were referred to as "Diggers."

When Captain John C. Fremont put into his journal "root diggers" for the Numic speakers around Salt Lake, and later "Digger Tribe" at Pyramid Lake, Nevada, he planted the seeds of the pejorative term "digger." Trap-

Living conditions of the Paiutes in the late 1800s. These Indians on Big Springs Ranch in Southern Nevada had not improved much since the days when the Ute Chief Walkara stole them and sold them to the Mexican ranchos in California and New Mexico. W.B. Lorton wrote in his diary in 1849 that these Piede (Paiutes) increase too fast and they sell their chidren for a "plug of tobacco."

per George Yount had harsh descriptions for people who ate "roots and reptiles, insects and vermine [sic]."[9] In fact, he said, "they almost burrow into the ground like a mole and are almost blind to everything comely" and are the "lowest dregs of humanity." They are the "worst type of savage I have seen" and they "abound with vermin." These Indians then became what was considered "valueless" in respect to treatment.

Another trapper Jedediah S. Smith—who owned two black slaves for awhile in Missouri—was just about as derogatory toward the Paiute-type Indian. They were the "most miserable of the human race." "Nearly naked, dirty, willing to eat anything that crawled or hopped or ran on the ground...poor people." "These wretched creatures go out barefoot in the coldest days of winter. They call themselves Pie-Utaws..."[10]

When Spanish families needed workers, either field hands or domestics or for the labor-intensive sheep raising and wool blanket industry, here close by were these "lowly" Indians, valueless people who could be marketed to the Spanish, Mexicans and later Americans. Under Spanish control captive prisoners could always be sold; captives of Spanish raids belonged to the victors as sort of extra pay, rewards for service to the Crown. Victims of allied Indian raiders were readily sold to Spanish settlements. So were captives taken by Indians in aggression by one Indian tribe against another. These too found a market. That market tied in with horse trading.

When the Spanish occupied New Mexico and later a third of California, the dynamics of Indian culture changed. Spanish values often conflicted with those of Native Americans. Indians traded furs for horses, guns, ammunition, steel pots and knives. The Spanish, like other European nations, had different sets of concerns: establishing secure settlements, developing land, saving souls, converting natives to become Christians and eventually to become citizens of the Spanish Kingdom, obtaining wealth, maintaining peace with the original "owners" of the land, and having the comforts of their ideal civilized society in Spain.

Abusive treatment of Pueblo Indians and growing resentment on the part of many Pueblo natives finally erupted in a rebellion, revenge and expulsion of Spanish colonists out of New Mexico to El Paso area. Though Indian rebel leader Popé and other Indian leaders burned churches, killed priests, and tried to erase Spanish culture, the Catholicness in hundreds of aborigines never died.[11]

Popé, however, became ruthless , becoming more controlling, causing loyalties to divide various pueblos. Popé had the habit of choosing the most beautiful women for himself.

On one attempt to reconquer New Mexico, the Spanish captured Zía Pueblo, killed 610 and took 70 slaves when they withdrew to El Paso.

Governor Don Diego Vargas, the implacably cruel but skilled negotiator and clever strategist, used much of his own money to effect the resubjugation. In 1693 when Tano Indians, who occupied the houses at Santa Fe, rebelled again, Vargas sold 400 Tanos into slavery. Silver mines in Mexico constantly required new workers, thus providing a continuing market for slave labor. Spaniards had up to 160,000 Indians working in those mines in the mid-1500s. The mines were sometimes a killing zone. Indians died of smallpox and measles and abuses. Working in dark shafts and mercury-poisoned reduction plants killed workers by the thousands. More Indians had to be shipped in. Labor-gangs under the *repartimiento* system allowed for only 2-4% of Indian work force in a village to be obligated to be sent to the mines. Spaniards abused or ignored the percentages. Obviously mine owners welcomed Vargas' prisoner workers.[12]

Independent Hopis, however, had so much hatred for the "slave church," as they called the Catholic church, that they resisted Spanish attempts at reconciliation. Memories festered in the hearts. They still remembered the unfairness of Oñate's conquest in 1590s. Though this brutal incident undoubtedly left a scar in the Hopi oral tradition, Franciscan missionaries eventually established three small churches on the Hopi mesas and baptized several hundred peace-loving and strongly-independent Hopis.

However, according to Hopi collective memory, actions of the missionaries caused resentments about losing some freedoms, undermining their religious traditions and values, dividing village loyalties, destroying symbols and icons, exploiting Hopi women, and punishing so-called infractions.

When the Pueblo Indian Popé led a successful rebellion in 1680, kicking the Spanish down the Rio Grande to El Paso, Hopis killed the "Castillas" priest, tore down the churches, and ridded themselves of everything Spanish—except sheep, horses and cattle.[13]

Internal harmony prevailed again.

Then Don Diego de Vargas reconquered New Mexico in 1692. Hopis resisted Spanish friendly overtures.

Suddenly in the fall of 1700, Spanish Padre Juan Garaycoechea appeared at the eastern Hopi village of Owatovi to reestablish the "Castillas" and the Catholic church, the slave church. Seventy-three villagers out of the estimated 800 population, agreed to be baptized or rebaptized. Then more accepted the Spanish.

The Pueblo split again. A delegation traveled to Santa Fe to ask for religious toleration and the governor refused. Complaints spread to other independent villages: people in Owatovi were not safe outside after dark because of criminals, Hopi religious artifacts were destroyed, decay of spirit set in. Baptized Hopis moved to the north side of the mesa near the newly-built church. Anti-Spanish aborigines disappeared; even wives of Hopis were not exempt from sexual abuse, and anti-Spanish clans moved in with fellow clansmen in other villages.

Finally Tapolou, chief of Owatovi, went to Oriabi and Walpi for help to rid the town of the infectious evil. Owatovi, his own village, he said, must be destroyed.

Other villagers agreed to destroy the evil during the night before Soyál, the Winter Solstice celebration. When the attack started, key men of Owatovi would be in the kiva preparing for the celebration; fires would be burning for the morning cooking. Hopi leaders told their warriors, "...the women and maidens you take; the men and old women you may kill"; they were to divide children and younger women among attacking villages.

Owatovi leader Tapolou let the warriors in the wooden gate. They carried weapons, cedar-bark torches, and bundles of creosote branches. Immediately they took the ladder out of the kiva, shot arrows into the kiva and threw in lit creosote branches, set fire to the firebrands and threw them into the kiva along with all the dried chili bundles hanging on the houses. The fumes killed the men. Then parties went through the village burning it down, killing Christians and old women, taking children and surviving women prisoner. More killing took place on the way to the other mesas. Though captives became slaves of other Hopis, some continued their clan rituals and celebrations while merging with their new villages. What happen to Tapolou? One story was that he went into the kiva and died with his people; the other claimed that he went to the Rio Grande and lived in another pueblo.

Warriors reentered burned out Owatovi the next day and broke everything usable: pots, metates, utensils, clothes. For 300 years Owatovi remained a dead, unused village on Antelope Mesa. Though stories about its destruction by its own people differed, Spanish and Hopi versions are basically the same. Fratricide it was, sacrificing one's own people for one's deep value convictions. The massacre was, however, traumatic with embarrassment and guilt lasting to the present time.[14]

The Spanish and later Mexicans left the Hopis pretty much at peace and independent.

In 1832 a group of Mexican soldiers (maybe militia) and Indian allies came to the plaza in Oraibi.

Supposedly (but very unlikely) they thought it was a village of Navajos. They camped by the water in the plaza and the Hopi gave them food. Suddenly Mexicans blew a brass horn and attacked Oraibi, killed a few people who resisted and shot them as they came out of the kiva. Hopis killed two raiders but saw a father shot while trying to save his son from capture. They witnessed another scalped and the capture of 14 children and a few women. One was the young wife of a man named Wichvaya. Castillas drove off hundreds of animals. They walked the prisoners to Santa Fe and repeatedly raped the young wife. They sold the captives into slavery and disposed of the stock.

Wichcaya, husband of a captured woman, and a few other Hopis went to see the governor in Santa Fe. The New Mexican governor with his military captain helped get the slaves back. One 7-8 year-old boy named Butterfly Wings Painted, sold to a couple in La Junta who had no children, was returned. The couple named him Tomás and fell in love with the new child so much that they cried when they had to return him. They had treated him so well the captain let the Mexican couple go. After hugging Butterfly Wings Painted they left crying. He later married another returned captive his own age named Corn Girl.

The returned wife, however, was so distraught that when she saw her husband Wichcaya again, she covered her head with her blanket. She had been sexually assaulted and hid her face in shame.

After their return to Santa Fe, the captain found these "soldiers" guilty and punished them for raiding peaceful Hopis instead of Navajos. He allowed the Hopis' children to witness the punishment. According to writer Frank Waters, the punishment was as follows: Some stood in front of graves they dug and were shot; others were dragged to death by horses; still others had iron balls with spikes tied to their legs so that spikes dug into their feet.

After the reconquest of New Mexico by Governor Vargas in 1692, except for this 1832 incident the Hopis, "so fanatically peaceful and stubborn, were never reinvaded...."[15]

During the 18th century Spanish colonists in New Mexico had a symbiotic relationship with periodically hostile Native Americans around the settlements. When there was peace, both the Spanish and Indians benefited from trade. A tradition that evolved from Spanish colonization movement north from Mexico City was the trading fair. Don Fernando de Taos reportedly held the first official annual trade fair in 1732 in the Taos Pueblo. It gathered traders from the Apache, Ute, Navajo, Comanche and Pawnee. Someone recorded that in 1760 Comanches brought 60 captured women and children--slaves to sell at the fair.[16] Slavery permeated Native American culture in the Southwest, and the Spanish expanded slavery in New Mexico and California.[16]

The returned Hopi wife of Wichcaya was so distraught that when she saw her husband again, she covered her head with her blanket. She had been so sexually assaulted by New Mexicans in 1832 and sold into slavery that she hid her face in shame. Original drawing by Kathy Kellar.

Three Chemehuevi Indians, living in the Mojave Desert for about 5,000 years, survived Indian slave trading by moving away from the Old Spanish Trail and key water holes. Notice recurved bow to the right, a most powerful Indian bow. The Chemehuevi occupied the eastern Mojave Desert and on the Colorado River near Parker. Painting is from Mollhausen in Ives Report, p. 54, Plate III.

The Mojave Indians and Slavery

The Mojave Indians[1] at one time occupied part of the eastern Mojave Desert from the Mojave River to and including the Colorado River but later resettled in several villages north and south of Needles along the Colorado River. Here they became adept at raising muskmelons, watermelons, corn, beans, crude wheat, and even cotton. They became middlemen in a trade that extended from the Hopi pueblos in Arizona and New Mexico to the coastal Indians around the present cities of Santa Barbara, Ventura, and San Gabriel. Their network of routes had a branch that went as far north as Bakersfield where the enterprising Mojave went to trade.[2] A branch of the Mojave River Trail later became known as the Old Spanish Trail, then the wagon route of "49er" fame, and still later part of the Salt Lake-Los Angeles freighter and mail route.

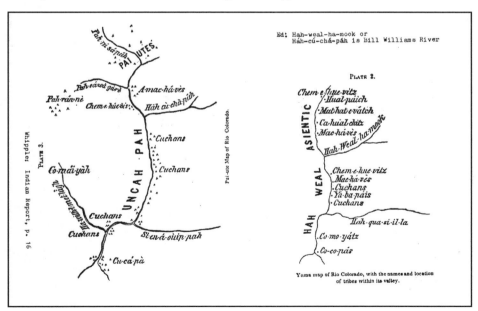

Left map, A Paiute map of the Colorado River sketched by Indians in Lt. Whipple's "Indian Report" 1854, p 16; on the right is the Yuma (Quechan) map. Pah is the Uto-Aztecan word for water. Notice Bill Williams Fork is Hah-ai-cha-pah and Hah-weal-ha-mook respectively. Notice too the spellings of Chemehuevi, Quechan, Mojave and Cocopah on each map

In order to visualize the ancient trade system of the Mojave Indian, one must read the accounts of the Spaniards who traveled the Mojave Desert. The first Spaniard to do so was Pedro Fages who in 1772 was looking for runaway soldiers and unhappy neophytes who were not slaves *per se*, but were sometimes used for involuntary colonization and service. Disgruntled coastal Indians began using the inland deserts of California for escapes from missionary life.[3] Little is known of Fages' experiences in the Mojave Desert, but he skirted inland valleys east of the Coast Range, thus seeing the interior deserts of California from eastern San Diego County, through San Bernardino area, Cajon Pass, Antelope Valley, and back to the coast by way of San Luis Obispo.

The second Spaniard who entered this desert fortunately recorded his observations in his diary. Fray Francisco Hermenegildo Garcés in 1776 traveled from Sonora up the Colorado River to the Needles area; and then with Mojave Indian guides he continued on the Mojave Indian Trail along the Mojave River and across the San Bernardino Mountains to the San Gabriel Mission. Father Garcés is credited with alerting California and Spanish authorities to the importance of the Mojave Indian Trail.

Even before reaching the Needles area, Garcés noted the Mojave Indians' practice of obtaining slaves.[4] In fact, the good padre's first encounter with the Mojave resulted in the purchase of two captive women slaves whom he later released and sent back to their own villages. Garcés bought the women as he was traveling up the Colorado River from the Quechan (Yuma) villages toward the Mojave villages. The Mojave received word of the Spanish visitors among the Quechan, and, being an inquisitive people, approached the country of their southern friends to satisfy their innate curiosity. Garcés shared his provisions with the Mojave party and discovered they had with them two captive Jalchedun *(Halchidhoma)*[5] women. It took some insistent bargaining before Garcés succeeded in purchasing the captives with what he termed "a poor horse and some other small presents." After five more days traveling up the river toward the Mojave villages, Garcés sent the two women slaves home with an old interpreter who had been instructed to assure the *Halchidhoma* of the missionary's friendship. Father Garcés had principles of humanity not frequently encountered among Catholic orders throughout the new world during the eighteenth century. His job, of course, was to save souls; and to do this he attempted to show each group of Indians of his and Jesus' "love" for them.

OLIVE OATMAN.

Olive Oatman, captured by the Yavapai in Arizona with her sister Mary Ann, then the Mojave bought the girls in 1852 for blankets, beads and horses. Notice the chin tatoos done by the Mojave. Mary Ann died of starvation in capivity.

The origin of slavery among the Mojave Indians was undoubtedly connected with their warlike operations. The practice may have evolved from simply killing their enemies to that of using those captured for work and/or trade. During a long prehistoric period, they had captured or traded for women and children whom they took back to their villages along the Colorado River. Mojaves used slaves to assist with the labor-intensive cultivation of crops planted in the rich soils of the overflow of the Colorado River. Sometimes captured children were permitted to grow up and live as Mojave. Slave women were often adopted, tattooed at puberty, and even married Mojaves. In some instances they traded slaves to other tribes, killed them, or tortured until death resulted.

Mojaves purchased Olive Oatman and her sister Mary Ann from the Yavapai Apache in 1852 for some blankets, beads and horses. Olive was a white slave of the Mojave for approximately four years during the mid-nineteenth century. After her return from captivity Olive Oatman met Rev. R. E. Stratton, and they wrote her story "in a sensational but imprecise, wordy, vague, emotional and pious" story. [5]

When sold to the Mojave Indians, Olive and Mary Ann lived with a chief, his wife and daughter. Since they lived with a chief's family, they were basically treated well. There was though a period of starvation, and Mary Ann died. Olive related not only her own experiences, including being tattooed, but also the tribe's supposed custom of killing a slave as a sacrifice should any member of the tribe be killed in battle—this may or may not be true. Since one Mojave told her that her "life must pay for the first (Mojave) that might be slain," according to Stratton, Olive Oatman feared the return of a war party against Cocopahs. She was relieved when all Mojaves returned safely, bringing in several Cocopah slaves.[6]

Slaves were often tortured and killed if they attempted to escape and were recaptured. When one mature Cocopah woman escaped for two days and was caught, she was horribly crucified, used as a shooting target, was a recipient of derision, and finally burned.[7]

A Mojave subchief had two Cocopah captive girls, and when his father became deadly sick, he killed one girl. When he returned to camp and found that his father had passed away, he killed the other girl and cremated her so she could be in the spirit world with his father. He also burned his father's bark garments, horse, and possessions to be used when he went to Awikwame, Spirit Mountain.[8]

According to Mojave informant Chooksa Homar who narrated the story of a small war with the Cocopa in the 1850s, the Mojave killed three men and took two Cocopah sisters as captives. They brought the prisoners back to the Mojave Valley and gave them to a leader in the southern part of the valley, had a water purification ceremony, and adopted them into the Mojave tribe. One sister named Orro, meaning "night hawk" in Mojave, married and had two children, a boy and a girl. The son and Orro were still alive in the Parker Reservation in 1903.

Though American soldiers had occupied the Yuma area for several years and continued to try to make peace within the tribes, fights still continued along the Colorado River. Homar said, as he recalled almost 50 years later, that maybe if these girls married and had children, half Mojave, half Cocopah, that may help create peace between these two tribes. Soon there was peace, though probably due more to American soldiers stationed at Yuma than mixed children. The Mojave escorted the unmarried sister to Yuma where the military had a ceremony of the Cocopah happily receiving one of their missing daughters.[9]

Stratton has been criticized for the Oatman book being over dramatized to fit into the romantic mode of the middle 19th century. It was a bit too exaggerated and the mood was titillating giving the impression that Olive was closer to a young adult rather than a child of 11-12 years. For example, Olive probably would not have used the lines "living in all the filth and degradation of an unmitigated heathenism" or described Mary Ann's death as "fading, withering, and wasting at the touch of cold cruelty."[10]

When Mojaves returned Oatman in 1855, they also returned a Mexican slave, freeing her also.

Judging from her interview with Major Martin Burke after the Mojave brought her to Ft. Yuma, she was treated quite well in the hands of the Mojave.[11]

Irataba, Chief of the Mojaves. This line-cut portrait and article are from Harper's magazine, vol. 8, February 13, 1864, p. 109. Photo courtesy of Smithsonian Institurion of National Anthropological Archives, Neg# 43,934. Irataba visited President Lincoln in 1864.

Here were some of Major Burke's questions on March 1, 1856, and Olive's answers:

> Burke: Whilst with the Apache (Yavapai, often called the Mo jave-Apache or Yavapai-Apache) did they use you well?
> Olive: No, they whipped me.
> Burke: How did the Mohave treat you?
> Olive: "Very well," she answered in a pleased manner.
> Burke: Was Mary sick? Or how did she die?
> Olive: Starved.
> Burke: Did the Mohave give you plenty to eat?
> Olive: Yes.
> Burke: What did you eat?
> Olive: Wheat, pumpkin, and fish.
> Burke: Musquite [sic] also?
> Olive: Yes.

Historian Richard Dillon in 1981 discussed the possibility and rumors of Olive Oatman having two half-Indian children. There was no evidence of that.[12]

Lieutenant A. W. Whipple visited the Mojave while Oatman was captive. Neither knew the other had been in the Mojave villages. Whipple noted when he was traveling through the Mojave villages in 1854 that "several sad looking fellows in the crowd were slaves." An Indian war captive was considered a disgrace. Even if he were to be returned to his tribe, his family might treat him with disdain.[13]

Yuman speakers (Hokan language) on the Colorado River from the Grand Canyon to the Gulf of Mexico had centuries of slavery with tribal enemies and alliances: Mojave and Quechan versus Halchidhoma and Cocopah, for example, and later upper tribes having to ward off slave raids of the Utes, Navajos and the Spanish. In Sheridan's book *Paths of Life,* the authors have a Smithsonian photo of two Cocopah men next to an Apache captive who became a Cocopah wife for the rest of her life. The Quechan developed such a hatred for the Halchidhoma on the Colorado River, and evidently such a like for their women and children that in the 1830s, surviving Halchidhoma families left their Colorado River homes and fled to Magdelena, Sonora.[14] When an epidemic ravaged them in

Mexico, survivors fled again to the Gila River to live by their Maricopa allies. With or without the presence of Europeans, Indian slavery was rampant in the old Southwest.

Mojave Indian bride and groom, taken around 1900. Notice face painting may be for the marriage. Courtesy of Los Angeles County Museum.

Luli-pah and Sowatcha. Two Mojave women photographed by Ben Wittick, date and location not recorded. Reproduced as "Fig. #7" Shufeldt's *Indian Types of Beauty,* **1892.**

California Slavery under Spain and Mexico

On the western portions of the Mojave River Trail, changes occurred with the advent of the Spanish settlements in California. Mission San Gabriel, established in 1771 prior to any journey of whites over the Mojave Desert, had considerable influence over the Indians of the Mojave Desert. Missionaries reeled in surrounding natives "by the mouth (with food)," but early records indicated that more than food and Christianity brought Indians into the missions. The Spanish used force.

Soon after the Spanish established Mission San Gabriel, discord erupted because a soldier outraged the wife of an Indian chief. The poor Indian objected; and besides losing his mate, he lost his life and then his head, which was impaled on the point of a long lance and placed near the stockade of the mission as a warning to all Indians. A padre later had the head returned to the natives, and Commandante Pedro Fages took the offending soldier to Monterey so he would be removed from the sight of the Indians whom the padre wished to attract to the mission.[1] Atrocities occurred. A few Spanish soldiers attacked an Indian village near a mission, stealing food and raping women. News spread through southern California making it difficult for recruiting new converts.[2]

These unhappy incidents caused Indians to stay away from the missions for a brief period, but the missionaries used strong persuasion and every possible kindness and the soldiers probably every kind of brutality to bring them under the mission yoke. Within ten years, Mission San Gabriel could count 1,019 neophytes. Hugo Reid, an early Scottish settler in Mexican California, who had married a southern California native, described the severe measures employed by the soldiers in recruiting converts to the mission.[3]

Since Indian death rates at missions were atrocious, missionaries needed to recruit more neophytes. They sent soldiers on expeditions at various distances from the mission where they captured whole villages of Indians, whipped them, and drove them back to the mission. Spanish and later Mexican priests forced Indian men, according to Reid, to make submission to the priests, and young children and infants were baptized. Priests separated Indian men from their wives until males requested baptism and had a "true" marriage performed.

Even Indians who were not brought to the mission suffered, despite the protestations of the priests. Fray Zephyrin Engelhardt stated that soldiers left the mission on horseback and traveled many leagues to villages where they drove off Indian men and lassoed women to satisfy their lust.[4] This too could be considered a type of slavery practiced in the inland valleys and deserts of southern California, a type of slavery that rivaled in scope the prehistoric slavery engaged in by the Mojave and other Indians.

Treatment of Indians at the California missions had other repercussions in the west. Indians continued to die off in the missions, and countless Indians fled to the hills and to the interior valleys. They, in turn, changed the value system and experiences of the interior Indians. Except for natives who were rounded up and forced into the missions, they were generally free to join a mission or not; but if they became attached to a mission, they could not leave without permission. Four hundred neophytes ran away from Mission San José on May 15 and 16, 1827.[5] Runaways were often hunted down. If a band of Indians was caught harboring runaways, the band was punished. These attitudes angered interior Indians. Within a mixture of runaways and native Indians, alienation grew between Indians and the Spanish culture.

Over the years cattle and horses bred and numbers expanded tremendously. After Mexico won its independence and took control of the Southland, it permitted trade with foreigners. Cow hides readily sold to Boston ships and became a basis of exchange, i.e., money. Wild horses abounded in the hills and they too spread to the inland regions. Certain Indians incorporated the horse into their lifestyles for riding, eating, stealing and trading. Since cattle hides served as cash for missions and ranchos, horses were often rounded up and slaughtered so cattle could eat the grasses.

Besides the incentive for profit, justification for horse-thieving operations might partly caused because Mexicans themselves slaughtered thousands of wild horses during the 1820s. José Del Carmen Lugo remembered when the ranchers rounded up thousands of wild and tame horses in three corrals near Los Angeles. Lancers stationed at corral exits killed horses not claimed; they cured the hides, but left the rest of the animals to rot. Even as late as 1837 the Los Angeles Ayuntamiento granted permission to the rancheros south of Los Angeles to build a corral at Serra de San Pedro to kill wild horses. H. H. Bancroft stated that in 1828 San Gabriel Mission had 2,400 horses, not counting wild ones; but the number declined from 2,225 in 1831 to only 220 in 1834. Since secularization occurred in 1833-36, one might guess that the rancho horses increased as the Californians occupied mission lands and obtained the animals. Early California traveler Farnham hyperbolically stated ranchers killed fifteen thousand of these animals in one year on one rancho just to preserve grass for cattle. Surplus horses in California attracted adventurers and opportunists into California for the next 25 years.[6] Availability of Indians in California also attracted slavers.

Indians in California periodically stole other Indians. For example, those around Sutter's Fort practiced wife stealing. Chucumnes on the Cosumnes River raided Maidu for wives. John Sutter caught some raiders and returned 14 captive girls. Then he executed seven kidnappers. He rescued slaves, yet he gave two girls away as presents. He used Indians as gifts and workers to help alleviate his continual indebtedness. He also hired "his" friendly Indians out for money.[7]

Despite practices around Sacramento Valley, Indian slavery among California natives seemed not as prominent except with Northwest tribes like the Yurok who had an entrenched custom of slavery based on their economy and search for wealth. In California a slave cost one string of dentalia shells, while up at Nootka, where shells were more available, a slave might cost five strings. An owner might even buy a wife for his slave, and their offspring would belong to the Yurok owner. The Chinook Indians north of the Columbia River became trading middlemen north and south, east and west. They probably owned more slaves per capita than other Indians in the area and were partly responsible for dentalia shells from western Vancouver Island getting out to the Great Plains. California slaves and "slaves from wherever" were traded at Nootka for Nootka canoes.[8]

Horse stealing from the Californio ranches and missions expanded each year. When Indians of the Columbia River adopted the horse culture, it was not long before they discovered horses available in the interior valleys of California. By 1800, according to anthropologist Thomas Layton, Columbian River Indians made periodical raids into California from the north, buying or stealing the following: Indian slaves, horses, and California shells. Walla Walla Indians came from their homes in Washington to trade (and possibly steal) in the Sacramento Valley, purchasing Mexican blankets and vermillion. Anthropologist Jack Forbes said Shasta Indians made slave raids around California and they too took their prisoners to sell at the trade fairs at The Dalles and Yainax, east of Klamath Lake, Oregon. Klamath Indians raided Pit River Indians for slaves up until 1857 to sell in Oregon.[9]

The Dalles had for several centuries been a trade center. Located where the Columbia River cuts through the Cascade Mountains, it was a place where Plains Indians and Nez Perce traded throughout the summer, trade "reaching its peak in the fall" with buffalo robes and meat exchanged with coastal Indians and Great Basin Indians. The Klamath brought camus bulbs to trade. Coastal Indians traded dentalium and other shells.[10]

Then the horse became the focus of trading. Columbia River Indians received horses from the Shoshone Indians which changed their lives and the lives of the Northwest indigenes, and as a result northern California natives changed also. When the British and American trappers joined in trading, they brought muskets, ball, powder, and shot, copper and brass kettles, brass tea-kettles, coffee pots, blankets, scarlet and blue cloth, wire, and knives.[11]

Slaves likewise became an important commodity. Nez Percés and Cayuses met and traded slaves, horses and other products includ-

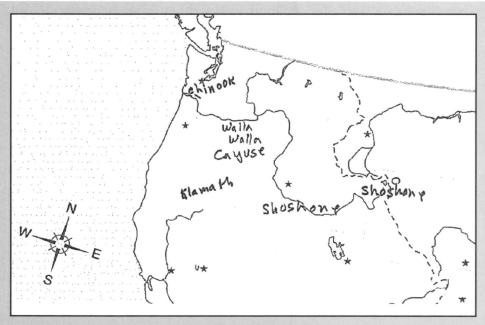

California-Oregon Tribes

ing goods produced by the Californios. The Dalles "was a great slave mart,"reported Lewis and Clark in 1806. California Indians, probably Klamath or Modoc, brought Pit River captives to another trade rendezvous at Yainax. Predatory mounted Shoshones from Idaho also came to Yainax with "Snake" Indians, that is, non-horse Shoshones, for sale.

In northeast Californi, Northern Paiutes had to pull away from the trail through Surprise Valley. That was one route Shoshones used to enter California and Oregon. Shoshones captured Northern Paiutes until Paiutes avoided them.[12]

John Work, Canadian trapper, in an expedition in the summer of 1832, found natives of Cow Creek on the upper Sacramento River very much afraid of horses and the slave raids of the Shasta tribe.

Because of the more established and warlike Plains Indians, Idaho Shoshones who acquired the horse were stopped from expanding into the Great Plains. They went into the Great Basin and preyed upon pedestrian Shoshone and Paiute. Displaced coastal California Indians, sometimes with horses, traveled to eastern California and Nevada to trade. Another horse and slave trading route developed in the northern and central Great Basin. Canadian trapper Peter Ogden in 1828 in the Great Basin found horse Indians wearing Mexican blankets and also discovering tracks of hundred of Indians and horses showing commerce across the Humboldt River Trail to and from the east.[13]

After Indians attacked Jedediah Smith's trappers in southern Oregon in 1828, the Hudson Bay Company helped Smith retrieve much of his furs and supplies. When he set out to find his equipment, he had 20 trappers and "nearly as many Slaves." He obtained another slave named Marion, a Willamette Indian left behind when his captors fled the approach of Smith. Smith also retrieved four of his runaway slaves who were "willing to reassume their former Situations." Another time Smith wrote about a slave boy attached to his party, "a Native of the Wullamette." How many of these were owned by Hudson Bay Company and how many belonged to Smith is unknown.[14]

Interior California Indians became middlemen by stealing horses from the coastal settlements and selling them to the Columbia River Indians. As early as 1815 José Dolores Pico from San Juan Bautista recorded his trip to the San Joaquin Valley where he counted at least 500 butchered horses at Indian camps he visited. As years went on, horses and Indian thieves advanced into the Sierra Nevada and eastern California and western Nevada.[15] Pico lamented all the best horses were being stolen "and in the Tulares (San Joaquin Valley) all ride, even the women; and regular fairs for the sale of horses are held there."

Mojave Indians continued to frequent their old trading haunts along the southern coast even though the Spanish discouraged such commerce. This conflict led to clashes between Mojave and Spanish. One of these occurred in Mission San Buenaventura in 1819 and ended in bloodshed and temporary slavery for aseveral Mojave. About twenty Mojave Indians crossed the Mojave Indian Trail and appeared at Mission San Buenaventura on May 29, 1819. Unfortunately, mission guards did not permit them to converse with Christian Indians or even visit the mission. In fact, they kept Mojaves in the guard house until ready to depart the next day. Evidently Father José Senan told the corporal the Mojave had done no wrong, but either it was too late or the guards still would not release the Mojave.[16]

The next morning one Mojave tried to leave and a sentinel struck him. Corporal Rufino Leiva and Mariano Cota came out of the church and tried to put the Indian in stocks, whereupon other Mojaves rushed to the rescue and slew the soldiers with clubs. The ensuing skirmish killed soldiers and nearly half the neophytes. Sergeant Anastasio Carrillo and fourteen soldiers from Santa Barbara Presidio arrived and pursued the ten Mojave who had fled. They caught four of them who were later forced these captives to work on Santa Barbara Presidio but eventually escaped. Officials sent reinforcement to San Gabriel as that mission was in the direct route from the Mojave River Trail.

Fray Luis Antonio Martinez of San Luis Obispo wrote to Governor Pablo Vicente Sola on September 17, 1819, that soldiers should be sent out on expeditions, especially before there was a union between the Christian Indians and the Colorado River Indians "who knew how to ride better than I." He added that, "They should be made to feel the arm of the Government."[17]

Governor Sola responded with alacrity. He ordered smiths at each presidio to put weapons in condition. Other personnel prepared dried meat and piñole, and officials issued clothing to soldiers. Californio officials planned and carried out three expeditions to the interior, one under Lieutenant Gabriel Moraga who left Santa Barbara in November 1819 with 354 cavalrymen, infantrymen, and artillerymen. He was to go to the Colorado River to ascertain if the Mojave were committing the atrocities reported at San Gabriel. If so, he was to capture the guilty and teach them a lesson they would not forget.

Descending the Mojave River to the present site of Victorville, searchers soon found evidence they needed: the remains of four mission Indians from San Gabriel, three from San Fernando, and some pagan Indians, all murdered by the Mojave. The Spanish held funeral services with ceremonies and processions before they buried the Indians beneath a large cross. Moraga and Fray Joaquin Pasqual Nuez renamed the place *Las Animas Benditas de Atongaibit* (Lost Souls of *Atongaibit*) [18] and named the Mojave River *"Rio de las Animas"* (River of the Souls or Spirits).

On the Mojave Indian trail, Moraga met a "pagan" Indian who had just come from the Amajaba (Mojave). He pressed this Indian into service to return with them as a guide to the Mojave villages on the Colorado.

At another rancheria called by the Vanyume *Sisugina*, the force found one adult Indian who had been killed by a club like the Mojave used.

They followed the trail downriver until they arrived at what Nuez called San Joaquin y Santa Ana, either Afton Canyon or the present Camp Cady site. In order to overtake the Mojave, Moraga and a select 14 rode ahead, traveling all day and part of the night until their horses could go no further.

They retreated--defeated not by the Mojave but by the desert trail where the Mojave River sinks into the sand.

Father Nuez told the story of Moraga's trip back to San Joaquin y Santa Ana:

"God so disposed that he [Moraga] found four pagans, three married, and a boy of thirteen or fourteen years, who were terrified, wandering aimless and unsettled with seven women and three children... whose father the Mojave killed and whose mother was taken away captive by them." Moraga sent his interpreter Indalario and the pagan he had impressed into service to look for the body of the father.

In following days Moraga discovered more bodies. One unfortunately was Indalario, the interpreter, found riddled with arrows. Moraga surmised that the same pagan evidently sneaked up a ridge and shot Indalario with arrows while he was eating his piñole; the pagan took Indalario's hat, lance and horse. Moraga assumed the pagan put the two elderly missing women on the horse and headed for the Mojave villages.

Moraga's little army arrived back in San Gabriel on December 14, 1819.[19]

The Mojave Indians continued their coastal trade but generally kept away from missions and Indians loyal to Spain (loyal to Mexico after

1821). They preferred to trade with renegade or runaway Indians. The Mojave Trail and interior valleys remained havens for fugitives from Spanish civilization. Capt. John C. Fremont encountered six Mojave on the Mojave River west of the present Barstow in 1844. They, one of whom was a Mojave slave who could speak Spanish, had just come from the San Joaquin Valley. From their conversations Fremont placed the name of the river "Mohahve" on his 1844 map.[20]

The Mojave captured many mission Indians who evidently preferred the treatment of the Mojave to the vicissitudes of the mission-presidio-rancho culture of California. Several Vanyume Indians lived with the Mojave into the 20th century.[21]

"Dwellings of the Natives of the Rio Colorado of the West." drawing by Baldwin Mollhausen, February, 1854 Neg No. 56,175. Notice the Mojave woman carrying a watermelon on her head, the men playing the spear and hoop game, the granary with the thatched roof, the winter homes. Courtesy of Smithsonian Institution National Anthropological Archives.

Mojave Runners. Place, date, and photographer not recorded; probably A. Frank Randall in the 1880s. Photo courtesy of Smithsonian Institution of National Anthropological Archives, Neg. #2801-b-10.

Mojave Chiefs Irataba (left) and Cairook and Mojave woman with child, from H. B. Moll-hausen painting, Ives Report, p. 66, Gov. Doc. Irataba, who went to Washington D. C., was 6' 3" and Cairook was 6' 6".

Paiute captive tethered to a tree eating grass.   Sketch by K. Kellar

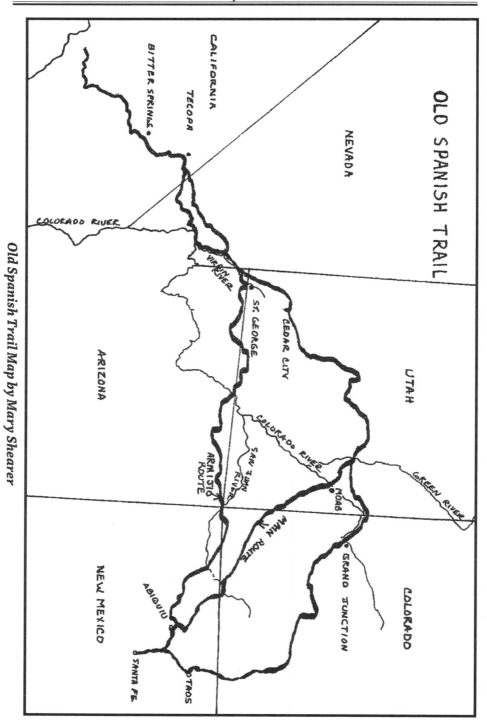

Old Spanish Trail Map by Mary Shearer

Continuing Slavery in New Mexico

Starting in 1829 in frontier towns like Abiquiu and Taos, New Mexicans initiated yearly mule caravans in the fall to California, heading west, following hundred-year-old trade routes into southern Utah and then through southern Nevada, hitting the Mojave River between present Camp Cady and Minneola Road. These New Mexican traders started what became known as the Old Spanish Trail.

Packing woolen goods from New Mexico to sell to Californios they left New Mexico in the fall when grasses came up. They wintered in California, trading their woolen goods for horses and mules.

When the spring grasses came up in California and the Great Basin, caravans reversed the route back to New Mexico. The Old Spanish Trail unfortunately expanded Indian slave trade between the two provinces of Mexico.

Elizabeth von Till Warren, in her article "Brutal Barter: Indian Slave Traffic in the Great Basin 1710-1888," analyzed records from New Mexico to help tell more of the story of the desert slave trade.[1] From records left in New Mexico, Warren tied Spanish and Mexican trade with trade across the Great Basin to California, thus filling in details of Indian slave trade in the Southwest. Mexican records showed that the Spanish had slaves from the end of the 16th century and trade continued even after the United States officially took over the area in 1848.

Buffers, such as military forts, were essential to the safety of established frontier towns and villages in order to protect them from threatening foreigners (including Indians). Both Spanish and English used forts to protect settlements from those who might attack them. New Englanders encouraged new settlements inland to buffer against the possible attacks and to warn of impending attacks from the French and Indians. Spanish colonists did the same thing by sending out a few families to occupy little mountain valleys ringing main settlements. The famous handicraft center of Chimayo in north central New Mexico was one of these small buffer settlements, now famous for its Chimayo blankets.[2] Most European countries sent out military patrols to deter attacks. The Spanish sent out missionaries to both save heathen souls and to buffer against surprise attacks—perhaps it was better that a mission be attacked and wiped out than a village—after all these martyred padres would go right to heaven. The subdued Indian pueblos on the perimeter of New Mexico helped as buffers, making Spanish settlements a little safer. Peace treaties and allies helped alleviate fears of the neighbors. . Basically some sort of outpost helped protect more established areas.

In the Americas these so-called outposts often became established towns or even cities and they, in turn, demanded new buffers for their protection. The Spanish in New Mexico utilized the system of genízaro pueblos on the frontier to protect against the Ute, Navajo, Comanche and Apache. The *genízaros* were detribalized Christianized Indians. Over the years, the Spanish freed captive Indians, such as Comanche war prisoners, who had become Catholic and worked as laborers or farmers, fitting into the Spanish culture. Many volunteered to fight against other enemies of the Spanish settlements. *Genízaros* might even end up with honors, land and slaves of their own as a reward. Authorities sometimes gave these alien residents pueblos to live in with attached land and basic freedom almost like a citizen of the Spanish kingdom. Fundamentally they lived in or around their genízaros pueblo, acted as a ready militia, went to church, farmed some land, married and raised a family. The children were Spanish citizens. The pueblo on the frontier, like Abiquiu on the border of land claimed by the Utes, became a buffer to deter Ute or Comanche attacks. Ex-Comanche captives helped the kingdom by living in Abiquiu.[3]

These *genízaros*, non-tribal Indians on the frontier, were often used as guides into Indian territories, workers on expeditions, participants on trading trips including slave stealing. One Ute *genízaro* raised by the Spanish was 70-year-old Manuel Mestas. According to Governor Joaquin Real Alencaster in 1805, Mestas served for 50 years as a Ute interpreter and was one who "reduced" the Utes to peace.

In the late18th century so much Indian trade with the Yutas occurred that the Catholic church and government leaders in northern New Mexico complained that slave trading could start another war with the Utes and would impede Catholic missionaries in saving souls of the Utes. They felt laws should be enacted to prohibit slave trading with the Ute tribes.

Commandant General of Provincias Internas Teodoro de Croix ordered a prohibition of trade with the "Yutas" in 1778. The punishment for disobeying the "bando" was incarceration, fines of 100 pesos, lashes up to 100, confiscation of trade items, and public service. Criers read the orders aloud in the public plazas. Alcalde-mayors Manuel Vigil of the Taos Pueblo and Antonio Baca of Villa de Albuqueque immediately published the law.[4] Generally local Indians and genízaros received the lashes and fines. In the typical double standard, guilty Spaniards received public work duties. Tradition, however, was too powerful especially with citizens from Abiquiu and Picuries Chama where their citizens were too tied to the Yuta trade to stop. French philosopher Baron de Montesquieu in 1748 said in Spirit of the Law that if a law violates the spirit of the law it will not be obeyed or cannot be enforced. After almost 200 years of New Mexican Indian slavery, there was too much tradition and habit to stop. Citizens knew too well the routes into the Great Basin. Some men participated in unauthorized punitive expeditions—to capture slaves.

Hispanic frontiersmen from Santa Rosa de Abiquiu stood before a magistrate in February 1783 for disobeying Croix's bando. This arrest was during the term of Governor Juan Bautista de Anza of Provincias Internas. Officials confiscated their supplies. Each trader had a variety of items to trade with the Indians, plus some had items belonging to town's people: almudes of flour, tobacco, almudes of corn, 25 awls, 10 knives, a sack of biscoches (biscuits), tobacco, horses and mules.[5]

Despite Spanish prohibition on dealing in Indians, especially the bando passed in September 1778 "forbidding settlers of Christianized Indians from visiting Utes for trade and barter" and another law in 1812, trading for Indian children continued.

In 1813 the Arze-Garcia party had been caught with newly purchased slaves. In a New Mexican trial, the leaders pleaded that they were "unwilling accomplices" and were practically forced to trade their goods for the Indians. When Governor José Manrique summoned them for an official inquiry, Mauricio Arze and Logos Garcia, both pled innocent. [6]

In the 1770s a Spanish official even arrested another pueblo official for giving trading permission to slaver Salvador Salazar and two other men In 1785 in San Antonio de Chama, Alcalde-mayor Garcia de la Mory authorized a trader to participate in illegal trading. Listed trading items were knives, awls, corn, tobacco, and horses to trade to Indians for hides, pelts, blankets and slaves. Ironically Mory himself became a silent partner when he gave the trader a box of knives to trade for him. Although the government arrested the alcalde-mayor, found him guilty, double fined him and assigned him public work service, later he was restored to his position of alcalde-mayor and as "Captain of war" for the same pueblo.[7]

Even though slave stealing, capturing, and selling were all illegal, there is much evidence that shows slavery was prevalent in New Mexico and the territories to the west, north and east of Santa Fe. From the end of the 17th century until after the Mexican-American War, there had been wars between the Spanish and Mexican colonizers and various groups of Indians. When Indians raided a Spanish village, they, of course, took women and children to use, trade, sell or hold for ransom. After the Spanish and later Mexicans, often with allies, raided the Navajo, Comanche, Ute or Apache, to avenge Indian attacks, they took captives sold them into slavery.

In just one small attack on the Navajo in 1839, for example, a few New Mexicans killed only two warriors but captured "six little slaves of both sexes."[8]

Baptisms illustrate the depth of the slave trade. From 1790-1819 there were 569 captives, mostly "Yutas," baptized north of Santa Fe, namely Abiquiu, San Juan, Santa Cruz, and Taos.[9] When the Catholic church baptized José Alvino Lucero in 1836, the mother Juana Maria stated that José was an Indian servant who had been "bought by Don Pablo Lucero." Also in Abiquiu, Miguel Antonio Gallegos bought and then baptized Antonio Rosa in 1822, a six-year old Ute. In Taos when the priest baptized José Cristóbal Martín, a 10-month-old Ute, the priest wrote, "the baptized is purchased from his father by Juana Martin."

Once in awhile court cases implied slavery existed. In Ojo Caliente, November 30, 1843, a plaintiff declared that "Antonio Jaramillo owes me an Indian and Pedro Espinosa a mule." Both of course were objects of property.[10]

"Uncle" Dick Wootton trapped extensively in the Wasatch Mountains of Utah and noted New Mexicans actively trying to buy slaves to sell in New Mexico. In fact, Wootton sent a load of furs with one slave party to sell in Taos, New Mexico.[11] Wootton said the Navajos and the New Mexicans had no qualms about purchasing their own "kith and kin."

Americans entered the trading in the Southwest after Spain lost control of her North American provinces. Mexico took control in 1821. Soon Missouri businessmen sent hundreds of thousands of dollars worth of goods to Santa Fe and Taos over the Santa Fe Trail. About two-thirds of these products were resold or shipped to Chihuahua on Camino Real. American trappers knew what sold to Indians: mirrors, flint, pots, axes, combs, pins, thread, beads, blankets, knives, buckles, gaudy jewelry, calico, tobacco, blankets and liquor, of course. But number one and two in sales or demand in the Southwest were horses and Indian slaves.

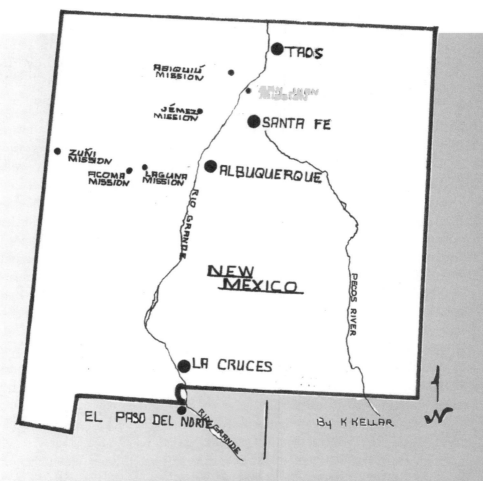

Tribes throughout New Mexico

A Strange Marriage—Utes and Mormons

Chief Wakara was a solid example of the mounted Utes of the times--[1] strong preying on the weak, stronger Utes taking advantage of the weaker Paiutes and the non-horse Utes.

While Wakara was active in Utah, Mormons (Church of Jesus Christ of the Latter Day Saints) occupied Salt Lake area and spread rapidly. Mormon policy was to make peace with neighboring Indian groups and try to convert them to their faith. Diplomacy worked fairly well. Along trading trails, according to Mormon and western historian Leo Lyman in his book *The Overland Journey from Utah to California, Wagon Travel from the City of the Saints to the City of the Angels,* Indians used the tribute system to exact meat, flour or presents from travelers through Indian territory. Mormons cleverly worked with the Indians to avoid travel loss and made the "tributes" beneficial to both Mormons and Indians. Travelers, Mormons and others, could even leave their cattle with the Indians at night for protection. In the morning Indians brought the animals back and received "pay" [instead of exacting tribute] which might be a weakened oxen or horse or hasty pudding.[2] Lyman's book examines in detail how this system worked to benefit both parties and helped build peaceful relations with the Indians in Utah and along the trails to the west.

Though the Saints felt Indian slavery hampered domestic tranquility in Utah, they had a more difficult time stopping the convoluted slavery traditions in the territory. Mormons punished Indians who attacked settlements of the Saints or who stole from them, yet they were more moderate in their revenge. When an Indian band kept raiding around the Provo River, Capt. John Scott with a Timpanogos Ute scout led a raid on the perpetrators at Battle Creek, killing the men and capturing the "squaws and the children" of the slain. Scott brought these captives to Salt Lake City where they were fed, housed and allowed to depart to friends among other Indians.[3]

In the winter of 1847-8 Utes offered two slaves for sale at old Salt Lake Fort. Mormons refused to buy, whereupon the Utes said since these children were captured in war, they would be killed at sunset if not sold. The Mormons bought one, but the Utes shot the other child at sunset. Later another two were offered for sale. The Mormons bought them. One of Wakara's bands near Provo told Mormons they had no right to stop slave trading. Wakara's brother Arapine grabbed a child by the heels and dashed his brains out on the ground. He told the Mormons that they had no heart; otherwise they would have bought the child and saved his life.[4] Later Indians brought two more children with the same demand, buy 'em or we kill them. The Mormons bought both children.

Again at Hot Springs, Utah, Indians wanted to trade a rifle for one slave girl. When the Mormons refused, the Indians tortured the girl in front of these Saints until one Mormon relented and traded his only rifle for the child. Two witnesses verified the account. Mary Ellen Kimball's journal of 1847 told of the horrible torture the girl endured, and Charles Decker's "heart was [so] wrung by witnessing such cruelty" that he gave up his gun. He gave the captive girl to his sister Clara D. Young, a wife of Brigham Young. She became Sally Young and grew up to be fine young lady, a well-liked Mormon, later marrying Pauvante Chief Kanosh. Unfortunately she was murdered by Kanosh's second wife. There were over 100 vehicles at Sally's funeral. The wife's murderer agreed to "expiate" her crime by starving herself to death, sitting alone in a crude shelter with a jug of water singing low tone sad songs.[5] Though Sally's life was cut short, she lived a good part of it in freedom.

Hafen and Hafen's classic *Old Spanish Trail: Santa Fe to Los Angeles* narrated several incidents about Wakara attacking some Piedes (Paiute) in 1853: they killed or wounded about twenty men and took as many women and children prisoners. Ute loss was "one man wounded and one horse killed." Hafen affirmed that Utes took these prisoners to meet the "Spanish [Mexican] traders." Mormon missionary Jacob Hamblin witnessed overt trading in 1854 when Sanpitch, another brother of Chief Wakara, went to the Paiutes on the Santa Clara River and traded for over a week. Hamblin said Sanpitch "bought three girls, giving one horse and three guns for them, and many beads. The father and mother of one of them cried on seeing their daughter go, but they had nothing to give them to eat, and the gun, her price, would help them get food. From the oldest girl, aged about 12, as she was carried off, I beheld the tears falling fast and silently, and my heart pained to think that she might become a slave to Mexicans."[6]

Indian Agent for Utah, D. Garland Hurt as late as 1860 wrote that the Py-eeds were so degraded that they sold their children for a few trinkets and bits of clothing, selling them to Mexicans and Navajos, buying quality Navajo blankets. Hurt estimated that "scarcely one-half of the Py-eed children are permitted to grow up in the band," most of those males.[7]

In the 20th century a friend and confidant of the Paiutes in Utah, Willaim R. Palmer, asked an old Paiute man why they traded their children. He answered "...they could make more children but they had nothing else to trade for horses and guns." Palmer related poignant stories told to him like that of a Paiute mother who followed a caravan for days for an opportunity to steal her child back. Another story about a captive girl who was told by a local Indian to run away at a certain point, hide in the day and travel by night, go to nearby village and he would marry her. She escaped and found her future husband—thus a beautiful love story and also an escape from a life of servitude.[8]

These sordid events happened mostly out of sight of the Utah Mormons, occurring despite the Mormon attempts to stop Indian slave trade in their territory. But eventually Mormons were instrumental in helping end involuntary servitude in the Southwest.

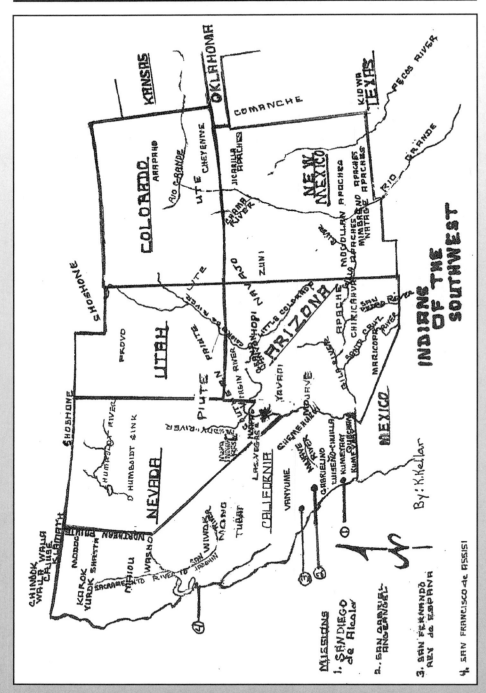

Indians of the Southwest

Glimpses of Mexican Slavery in California

The Spanish government tried to make it easier for children of racially mixed groups to have full Spanish citizenship. By custom and practice, especially in Jesuit jurisdiction, after ten years as a mission the mission became a parish church, the land was allocated to each Indian family and these adults were citizens of Spain. Spain, however, expelled the Jesuits in 1767, and Franciscans did not follow these guidelines, some missions never becoming parish churches, especially in California. In 1796 Governor Borica in a letter noted that the missions were supposed to function for ten years and then be turned over to the clergy. Borica said, "but those [Indians] of New California will not reach the goal in ten centuries; the reason, God knows, and men know something about it."[1]

A few years later a Franciscan maligned the same Indians he was supposed to love and care for as a shepherd cares for his sheep. In 1816 San Francisco mission father characterized Indians "as lazy, stupid, jealous, gluttonous, timorous"; he added, "I have never seen any of them laugh, I have never seen anyone look in the face....They have an air of taking no interest in anything."[2]

Under the *Plan de Iguala* pronounced on February 4, 1821, by the Mexican leader Agustín de Iturbide at the end of Mexico's war for independence from Spain, if an Indian child was born after a marriage, there should be no citizen discrimination: "All the inhabitants of New Spain, without distinction, whether Europeans, Africans, or Indians, are citizens of the monarchy [Iturbide] with a right to be employed in any post, according to merits and virtues."[3] Supposedly "birth" didn't matter to the Mexican government, but the reality was birth did matter for years to come.

The first American who traversed the Mojave Indian Trail gave evidence as to how missionaries treated Indians at the San Gabriel Mission in California. Jedediah Smith and his trappers entered the domain of the Mojave Indians in 1826 and were hospitably treated. The exhausted trappers remained in the Mojave village on the Colorado River for two weeks, resting and buying melons, corn, beans, pumpkins, and a little wheat. They even purchased horses from runaway Indians (who spoke good Spanish) who had stolen them from the Mexicans in California. Smith hired two Indians to guide him over the Mojave Desert to San Gabriel Mission.

Even though the surprised Mexican authorities treated Smith and his rugged trappers with suspicion, at San Gabriel padres welcomed the Americans with "good old whiskey," wine, and "sigars" and feasting. The next day they had tea, bread and cheese, gin and water, and then dinner. The two Mojave Indian guides were treated in another way, however: they were locked up in the stockade.[4] Officials sentenced one guide to death; the other died in jail.

Harrison G. Rogers, Smith's clerk and second in command, recorded unpleasant treatment of Indians, who he felt were kept in a state of bondage as complete as slavery. On Sunday, January 14, 1827, four Indians who had been fighting and gambling were sentenced to thirty to forty lashes on the "bare posteriors." Another time five or six Indians were brought to the mission and ". . . whiped, and one of them being stubbourn and did not like to submit to the lash was knocked down by the commandant, tied and severely whiped, then chained by the leg to another Indian who had been guilty of a similar offence."[5] Rogers also became disgusted when he observed the Sunday routine. After church, which included music by an Indian band, the priest ordered meat be issued to the Indians. But he then threw oranges to a cluster of young women to see them squabble.

Many writers including J. Arguello in 1797 affirmed the negative treatment of the California mission Indians. When 30 Indians were interviewed as to why they ran away from Father   Danti and the mission in San Francisco, their answers gave harsh insight into mission life: One said it was because he wept over the death of his wife and child and was ordered flogged on five occasions by Father Danti. Another because he was sick. Another because his wife and one son died. One gave as his reason because he was hungry and put in the stocks when he was ill. One neophyte gave as his only reason homesickness. Another because his wife, one son and two brothers had died in the mission. One did so because his wife and son were fugitives and because he was continually being beaten. Another because the *alcalde* beat him all the time and he was made to work while he was sick. One simply because he was given a blow with a club. One because he was beaten when he wept for a dead brother. One said he did so in order to see his mother. One because his mother, two brothers and three nephews had died in the mission, all of hunger, and he ran away so that he would not also die. One because his wife sinned with a settler and the priest beat him for not taking care of her. The other statements were similar, mentioning either lack of food, deaths of loved ones, or harsh punishment.[6]

These affirmations reveal personalities connected with a few neophyte deaths. Mission Indian death rates were horrendous. Hubert Bancroft broke mission statistics into 10 year periods, more or less, some of which follow:

MISSION & DATE	BAPTISMS	DEATHS
San Luis 1790-1800	675	523
San Juan 1810-1820	735	755
San Francisco 1801-1809	1,978	1,530
San Miguel 1801-1809	666	605
San Carlos 1801-1809	454	586.[7]

The two prefect districts of Santa Barbara and San Diego [all the south] declined in neophyte population from 1821-1829 from 11,600 to 9,000, while the white population gained from 1,800 to 2,310.[8] Earlier, Mission San Jose had a gain for ten years starting 1806 from 1,247 to 1,332, but it took 1,724 baptisms to raise the population that much. Gov. Solá sent a report stating to the Viceroy in 1818 that from all the missions up to that time 41,000 Neophytes died out of 64,000 baptized.

Though no two missions were alike, Indians did not always have a pleasant mission experience. Death rates were much higher than birth or marriage rates. Work requirements were rigid. Neophytes rose at dawn; listened to mass, had breakfast of barley mush; lunched of a mush of barley, peas and beans; and dined (after divine service) on barley mush again. Depending upon the supply and the inclinations of the priests, there was some meat from the mission herds. This diet provided an estimated 2000 calories per day.

Men and women—even pregnant women—had to work. Some labor classed as hard work; for example, a man's quota was 40 adobe bricks or 28 roof tiles per day.[9]

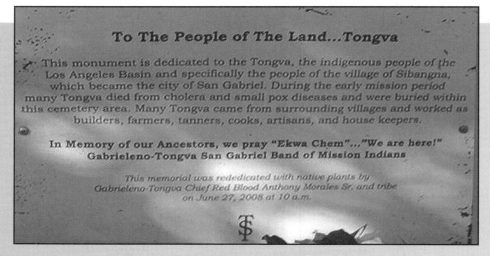

Tongva people of the Los Angeles Basin at the village Sibangna (San Gabriel). Most have gone the way of the earth, but a few are still here. Bottom sentence reads: "This memorial was rededicated with native plants by Gabrieleno-Tongva Chief Red Blood Anthony Morales Sr. and tribe on June 27, 2008 at 10 a.m." Though some of their ancestors were brought into the mission by force, today's survivors announce...We are here!"   *Photo by Walter Feller.*

Smith and Rogers commented further on this mission life. To help earn their keep, some trappers worked in the mission blacksmith shop. At the request of Padre José Bernardo Sanchez, Americans made a bear trap, and about a week later the priest asked Rogers to make a large trap to set in his "orrange garden, to catch the Indians when they come up at night to rob his orchard." Unfortunately for historians, Rogers neglected to record the statistics as to how many bears or Indians were subsequently caught.[10]

In defending California Missions, Father Maynard Gieger, G.F.M., said missions were not as bad as critical historians made them out to be. Santa Barbara Mission, Register # 1 showed that Indian deaths from 1787 to 1841 were 3,997, almost 75 per year. To this author that seems like a tremendous amount of Indian deaths especially considering secularization was almost complete by 1834.[11] Fewer Neophytes associated with missions after 1834.

Geiger put some blame on the Spanish and Mexican (mestizos) when he quoted Fray Ramon Olbers in 1812 who said the *gente de razón,* civilized citizens of Santa Barbara, were "lazy and so given to idleness that they know nothing else but to ride horseback, and consider all work as dishonorable....only Indians ought to work....They solicit the service of Indians for cooking, washing, working in the green garden, minding the baby, etc. Generally we missionary fathers allow[ed] the Indians to work for them."

Indians did not work that hard, said Geiger. They started work at 8 or 9 in the morning depending on the season, and quit for noonday meals. In the afternoon Indians only worked an hour and a half. Others with assigned jobs like brick or tile making or weaving worked longer. Field workers labored to about 3:45 p.m. Missionaries' attitudes toward Indians varied, but they were not always as sympathetic and as benevolent as the romantic age of the California Mission Period often portrays.[12]

Smith and his trappers saw firsthand the relationship between missionaries and mission Indians. Smith did not complain about their treatment as guests at the mission but did not approve of Indian treatment. The American trapping party left San Gabriel and went to the San Joaquin Valley to trap. Three trappers crossed the snowy Sierra Nevada and the dry deserts of Nevada to attend the rendezvous of trappers in Utah in 1827. Within two weeks Smith and a new crew of trappers were again on their way to the Mojave villages. Although the Mojave pretended friendship, they were actually bent on retribution for the loss of thirty to fifty warriors at the hands of Ewing Young and his band of trappers a few months before. When the Mojave helped Smith cross the Colorado River, they suddenly attacked Smith, killing nine of his nineteen men, all of whom were brutally slain. Two Indian women traveling with Smith (wives or friends of the trappers) were held by the Mojave as slaves.[13]

When Young's men returned to the Colorado River within the year, a Quechan Indian with the Mojave told him of the Smith massacre and offered to obtain one of the "beautiful" captives, for an adequate reward of course, but Young declined to ransom the "captain's squaw," meaning maybe trapper Sublette's or Smith's [?] woman. Young kept his dealing with the Mojave at a minimum. Thus the Indian ladies (wives or "friends" of the trappers) probably lived the rest of their lives with the Mojave.[14]

American and Canadian trappers entered the New Mexican environment and adapted to the slave stealing and barter. They already knew how to befriend a tribe and marry into or at least consummate a relationship with Indian groups.

When the price of beaver plews dropped in the late 1830s to about

$1.00 per pelt and it became more difficult to find fresh streams to hunt, the beaver-trapper business became less profitable. In 1829 a trapper could make from $600-800 a year. By 1838 the great days of trapping were over. Because of beaver hats going out of fashion and being replaced by silk hats, trapping had diminished to such an extent that suppliers needed only 25 wagons to supply the rendezvous and trappers brought in only 200 beaver pelts. One observer, Thomas J. Farnham, described the trappers' plight "in the desperate year of 1839-40, when the livelihood had been reduced to famine proportions...."[15]

Many trappers settled down to farm in California, some became businessmen in New Mexico, others went back home, and a few became scouts for the military or for explorers. A small group took advantage of lax law enforcement in Mexican California and went into the horse thieving business by raiding California for horses and mules.

A couple former trappers found a little profit in slave trading. According to a Methodist minister Reverend Joseph Williams, trapper Antoine Robidoux had "debauchery" with "the men among the Indian women" at Fort Wintey, Utah. Robidoux "collected several of the Indian squaws and young Indians to take to New Mexico and kept some of them for his own use. The Mexicans bought them for wives." Fremont said Navajos attacked Fort Wintey and carried off nine men and women. Fremont also commented that Canadian and Spanish *engages* [trappers] usually had a supply of women.[16]

These dauntless trappers not only recorded evidence of slave activity but also conquered the desert routes for others to follow. On the heels of these beaver men came Antonio Armijo who led the first New Mexican caravan in 1829-30 over what became called the Old Spanish Trail. New Mexicans finally completed the 1776 dream of Father Garcés' overland route between New Mexico and California. As he predicted, the road brought prosperous trade and pacification to some recalcitrant Indians. But it wrought disaster to bands of roving Uto-Aztecan Indians who could not protect themselves from aggressive traders who came through their formerly unmolested regions. The so-called Paiute Indians suffered at the hands of the increased travelers.[17]

The success of conquering the route across the Mojave Desert and the bright promise of the trade that the Mojave River Trail offered New Mexico and California were both soon tarnished by the malevolent proclivities of man. These tendencies were manifested in three ways: traders in Indian slaves used the route to carry contraband to and from California; New Mexicans, Utes, and Chaguanosos (thieves of many nations including American trappers) used this route for their clandestine avenue of approach and escape for their horse-thieving raids; and several California Indians continued to use the area as a haven after raiding Mexican ranchos and missions.

Slave trading in California was the least publicized of these three surreptitious endeavors. Buying and selling of slaves had been practiced in New Mexico in sundry forms since the seventeenth century. Even though Mexico made slavery illegal in 1829, slavery existed and continued in more subtle fashion: indentured servants, domestics, peons and the like. With a close examination of numerous documents left for posterity, one can find evidence that slave trading activity still persisted, some of which involved Southern California.

On July 13, 1824, California's provisional government passed a decree forbidding Indian slave trade. Yet slavery in various forms occurred both brazenly and surreptitiously. In the case of José Rocha when officials in 1833 tried him in California for purchasing an Indian boy from a New Mexican trader for 70 pesos, Rocha pleaded innocent because his intent was to adopt the boy, raise him as his own and as a Catholic. The same year in January, California land owner Ignacio del Valle reported to the *alcalde* in Los Angeles that New Mexican Francisco Vigil offered to sell an Indian boy. Valle turned down the offer because of fear of prosecution. Vigil left southern California before the *alcalde* could catch him.[18]

With New Mexican and Utah slave trading so ingrained in the New Mexican culture and in the trading life, one would naturally expect that more slave trading would be brought into California over the Old Spanish Trail. It was. New Mexican traders did many nefarious things in California: they sold liquor to Indians at Mission Conception (probably La Purissma Conception), they illegally entered Tulare (San Joaquin) Valley and incited Indians to steal horses and mules for them, they sometimes became so rowdy they had to be asked to leave and once were even escorted to the Cajon Pass, they both openly and secretly sold Indians to ranchers and maybe missions, they may have purchased Indians to sell on their return trip to New Mexico, and some New Mexicans sneaked into California without checking in. One can only guess what clandestine activities they undertook while wandering around unofficially. But one can imagine the untold sadness wrought by slave dealings.[19]

Brown and Boyd,[20] San Bernardino County historians, recorded the treatment meted out to the Cucamonga Indians during the rancho period which followed the decline of the missions. Governor Juan Alvarado granted Don Tiburcio Tapia in 1839 the Cucamonga Rancho. As was the custom of the times, Tapia believed that the Indian inhabitants of the land he received also belonged to him. Indeed, the *encomienda* system entrusted Indians who lived on land grants to the care of the one who received the land grant. This was especially true in California land grants after 1833 when missions became secularized and governors granted thousands of acres to favored Californians. Tapia, therefore, forced these quiet and industrious natives to build his buildings, plant his vines and orchards, and care for his livestock. As stock increased and vines and orchards were ready to bear fruit, Tapia brought in a number of Mexicans to do the work and forced the Indians to take refuge in the mountains and canyons. Don Tiburcio even employed guards to keep the nearly starving Indians from taking any of the fruits of their labors. He eventually sent his ranchmen out in force to hunt down and destroy the Indians as if they were just predatory animals. The *encomienda* system often led to the exploitation of the Indians by the *encomiendero*.[21]

During and after secularization (1833-36), instead of mission land being turned over to the Indians as was the policy under the Jesuits, governors put a *comisionado* (commissioner) in charge of each mission and later granted mission land to Californians. As with those allocated to Don Tapia, Indians were at the mercy of these new owners or off on their own to survive. Bancroft affirmed that for 5-8 years, missions were plundered because of corruption, greed, inefficiency, and incompetence. Neophytes ran off and worked for rancheros, and missions ended up having from 30 Indians to a couple hundred. Governor Chico, for example, used mission cattle and food stuff to pay debts. Officials loaned mission cattle to ranchos—never to be paid back. Tools were taken. Indians were exploited.[22] Missionaries portioned out land allotments to selected Neophytes, but few ended up owning land after a couple years. The system failed the Indians.

This treatment at missions and by new owners of mission land grants embittered California Indians. Runaway Indians continued to flee to the interior valleys (San Joaquin, Mojave Desert, and Colorado Desert [Imperial County today]) and a few waged war on settlements, especially in the San Diego area, through the Cajon Pass and the Pacheco Pass (east of Gilroy).Ironically they raided missions and ranchos for horses, supplies and Indian women. So much chaos existed that Christian Indians from Mission San Jose raided the interior valleys for gentile women. Sutter helped these gentiles defend against civilized Christian Neophytes.[23]

Col. Castro sent a huge force to Kings River region with instructions in a letter from the *alcalde* of San Jose to the governor stating orders were to "exterminate all male thieves from ages 10 years and up and capture all women and children." No extant copy of a report of the punishing trip exists except that Captain Estrada returned with 77 captives, mostly women and children.[24] Sounds suspect to this author. California in the secularizing years was a havoc for missions and Indians, both gentiles and Neophytes alike.

Don Benito Wilson, *alcalde* of Yucaipa, conducted two raids to quell Indians of the Mojave River area and one expedition to the lower desert. Susanna Bryant Dakin recorded such a raid in 1845, quoting from Wilson's own writing.[25]

Wilson asked Don Enrique Avila ". . . if he would join me with ten picked men and renew our campaign down the River Mojave. He answered that he would do so, *con mucho gusto*. He came forthwith, and we started for the trip, twenty-one strong.

"Some seven or eight days after we reached the field of operations, myself and Avila being in advance, we descried an Indian village. I at once directed my men to divide into two parties, to surround and attack the village. We did it successfully, but as on the former occasion, the men in the place would not surrender, and on my endeavoring to persuade them to give up, they shot one of my men, Evan Callaghan, in the back.

"I thought he was mortally wounded, and commanded my men to fire. The fire was kept up until every man was slain. We took the women and children prisoners."

A neglected account of Wilson's exploits against the Indians on the desert came from Juan Bautista Esparza, who accompanied Wilson on the two trips.[26] Wilson encountered and killed an ex-mission Indian named Joaquin, who had had his lip branded and his ear severed by the *mayordomo* of the San Gabriel Mission rancho at Chino. According to Esparza, this Joaquin was evidently a leader of the party at Resting Springs that attacked the Hernandez, Giacome, and Fuentes party of the 1844 New Mexican mule caravan and carried off two Mexican women. John C. Fremont's expedition came across the mutilated bodies of Hernandez and Giacome in 1844.[27] Joaquin obtained revenge for his mistreatment by the Mexicans; and he also secured women. How long Joaquin kept the captive women is unknown. Neither Esparza nor Wilson mentioned finding the Mexican women.

Esparza also said that some Indian women brought in by Wilson could speak Spanish. It remained a question for the Mexican authorities to ascertain whether they were induced to leave the missions or ran off on their own volition or had been released in the secularizations of the missions after 1833. Since Governor Pio Pico did not order any punishment of the women, chances were they were either forced to leave or were carried off by renegade Indians, or perhaps some of each occurred. What happened to the women and children after Wilson brought them to San Gabriel is also unknown. They were, in good probability, portioned out to Wilson's punitive party or to the surrounding ranchos as domestics, a euphemism for slavery.

At the Treaty of Guadalupe Hidalgo in 1848, ending the Mexican-American War, the Eleventh Article of the treaty tried to prohibit illegal raiding and slave stealing and selling across the two borders. Americans were to provide some security to prevent these illicit activities by attempting to restrain groups from entering Mexico to raid for slaves. The treaty prohibited Americans from purchasing or acquiring Mexicans or foreigners residing in Mexico (see Gomez in Chapter 9).[28] The treaty may have hindered the slave trading but hardly stopped it.

Don Benito (Benjamin) Wilson, later Mayor of Los Angeles and Indian Agent, led the California Mexicans in two expeditions in 1845 into the Mojave desert to quell Indian depredations, which included the stealing of women. Courtesy of Los Angeles County Museum.

Mission San Gabriel, one of many California Missions that intended to save souls but had negative results for thousands of Native Californians. Photo by Walter Feller.

Eye Witnesses on the Trail and in California

Other facets of this Indian slavery came from the travelers who kept records or diaries of their experiences on the Mojave-Utah branch of the Mojave River Trail. One of the first Americans to use the Mojave Trail after the Treaty of Guadalupe Hidalgo showed knowledge of the slave activity. Orville C. Pratt, who was sent to California by Secretary of War Marcy and President Polk in 1848, wrote that in Southern Utah the "Pah Eutahs" were afraid of the Mexicans because they often carried the Indians into captivity. Again at Las Vegas he wrote about the number of Pah Eutahs in the vicinity who ran away like wild deer.[1]

A diary kept by William B. Lorton on his trip to California in 1849 revealed the extent to which this selling of Indians took place. While Lorton was in Utah, before his trip across the Mojave River Trail, he noted that he met Ute Indian Chief Wakara, the "hawk of the mountains" and famous horse stealer and terror of the "Spanard and Pied."[2] Wakara made two trips into California and perhaps made many more as there were numerous reports of Utes raiding the outlying ranchos in the 1840s. The Pied Indians [Paiute] were in the depth of poverty, Lorton continued; they increased too fast, and for a "plug of tobacco" they sold their children into bondage to the Spanish ranchos or to the New Mexican traders on the Old Spanish Trail.

As early as 1835, Wakara had some dealings with Isaac Williams' Ranch (Rancho Chino which was once part of the massive Mission San Gabriel holdings), but the veracity of the quotation cannot be taken without challenge: "Indian Waker deals largely in Piede children and horse flesh, he agreed with Wms to purchase a lot of children and [when] the time came to receive them Wms had left, but, bound his successors to fill the contract, but this he (the successor) refused to do, so he [Wakara] assembled his men and proceeded to the place, now says he 'I want the number of children or your scalp.' They were given."[3]

As recompense for the "dishonesty" of the ranchero, Wakara stole one thousand head of horses.

In the 1844 census of Los Angeles, Rancho Chino recorded 67 Indians, 11 of which were listed as "washer women." Some of those could very well have been the Indians Williams supposedly sold to Wakara. [4]

Author Paul Bailey credited Wakara as being, by 1835, the "acknowledged and undisputed lord of the Mexican-Indian traffic in human flesh."[5] This cunning Ute chief, who only fifteen years later was baptized into the Mormon faith, took captive women and children from the weak bands of Shoshonean stock in Southern Utah, Nevada, and probably the Mojave Desert and sold them as slaves around Los Angeles. Depth was possibly added to Wakara's profits by seizing captives on his return trips to Utah; these, in turn, he sold to the Mexican traders around Santa Fe.

A little further south on the Old Spanish Trail, in Utah, Lorton noted in his diary that Indians came into camp with an infant captive which one Indian wanted to sell for a mule. Americans talked the Indians into cleaning the child's face, but declined the purchase.[6]

Besides Lorton, other Americans corroborated the evidence of slave trading. In 1849 Jim Beckwourth, who made a trip from Santa Fe to California delivering dispatches, commented on the "Pi-e-ches... who were hostile because of continual abduction of their squaws and children, whom the Mexicans employ as domestic slaves, and treat with utmost cruelty."[7]

T. J. Farnham, in his 1849 book *Life and Adventures in California with Travels in Oregon* revealed several facets of this illicit trading. He quoted Dr. J. H. Lyman, who came to California in 1842 with the Workman-Rowland party, as saying the "Paiuches" were fair game; for the New Mexicans had captured them for slaves for years and so did the neighboring Utes. Sometimes American trappers dealt in slaves because of the declining prices of beaver pelts after 1840.

"The price of these slaves in the markets of New Mexico," according to Farnham, "varies with the age and other qualities of person. Those from ten to fifteen years old sell from $50 to $100, which is by no means an extravagant price, if we take into consideration the herculean task of cleansing them fit for market."[8]

In Warren Beck's history of New Mexico, the price was put as high as $300 for a healthy Indian on the Santa Fe market.[9] It is hard to visualize such a high price in California since secularization in 1833 released thousands of mission Indians, many becoming homeless, raiding ranchos and Old Spanish Trail pack trains. Nevertheless, some slaves were brought into California by way of the Mojave River Trail or the Old Spanish Trail. In fact, the section of the trail from Las Vegas to the Mojave River had scattered bands of Panamints (Timbisha), Southern Paiute, Vanyume and Chemehuevis, all of which were small scattered villages of Numic or Takic speaking stock of Uto-Aztecan Language, often just referred to as Paiutes. No doubt a few New Mexicans, and perhaps Americans, succumbed to temptation and caught Indians, then sneaked the contraband into California. Dr. Lyman inferred as much when he cited how the Paiutes "pine away and often die in grief for the loss of their natural deserts," even when surrounded with the abundance of the settlements. One Indian brought into California continually refused to eat, moaned much of the time, and finally died.[10]

Chemehuevi Chairman Charles Wood stated, "Men, women and children were kidnapped and sold into the lucrative slave trade....Whole families might disappear never to be seen again and their genealogy lost." On August 6, 1853, Gwinn H. Heap cited another example of slave stealing. While accompanying the newly appointed California Indian Agent E. E. Beale to California over the Mojave River Trail, Heap wrote that annual expeditions were fitted out in New Mexico to trade with Pah-Utahs for children. José Galliego, a New Mexican employee of Beale, told Heap of it with *gusto*, recounting numerous anecdotes. Later when he saw a few Paiutes, "Galliego...rode up to Mr. Beale, and eagerly proposed to him we should 'charge on it like hell, kill the mans, and may-be catch some of the little boys and gals.'"[11]

Mexican records of Los Angeles further substantiated slave trading activity. The *Minute Book of the Illustrious Ayuntamiento Census of 1844* for Los Angeles and the surrounding ranchos listed nine "Payuche" Indians, ranging from ages nine to 13, and one three-year-old "Payuche"; whereas in the 1836 census there was not one "Payuche" listed.[12]

The Los Angeles Plaza Church death records up to 1850 contain scattered reference to Paiutes, Utes, or Indians from New Mexico:

1831   Maria Yuta, Indian child

1843   Dolores Palluche, of the Colorado River.
         Married as a gentile, baptized a few days ago

1845   Santiago, Indian child of Maria de la Luz, Indian
         from New Mexico

1846   Maria Conception, Indian adult "de nacion Palluche" and
         "Hija politica" (adopted daughter) of Don Ignacio Coronel

1848   Maria de Jesus, Palluche, adult [13]

Only one Paiute marriage, however, was recorded in the church records up to 1850, and that was Juan Andres Rodriquez, from New Mexico, who married Maria del Rosario, "Palluche," from La Puente Rancho.

No story better illustrated the atrocities toward the Paiute by the New Mexicans than the eye witness account of Michael White. White, an

A cemetery at San Gabriel where at least 6,000 southern California Indians died and were buried. Now only a small sign marks the burial ground. Diseases, abuse, and difficult mission life created the high mortality rate. Photo by Walter Feller

Englishman who became a Mexican citizen, known as Miguel Blanco, left Los Angeles in 1839 with a New Mexican caravan under the leadership of Tomas Salazar. White traveled for adventure and profit, planning to sell a few coveted California mules in New Mexico. Ten-peso mules in Los Angeles brought fifty pesos in New Mexico.[14]

The anticipated profits soon turned to revulsion. The caravan rested by a lake called San Jose (later called "Beggars" by White) probably in Utah. He told his partner to look after the horses and mules while he rode around the country.

When he heard shots, he rushed over the hill to find the New Mexicans had surrounded a rancheria of Indians. White saw one Indian boy with his arm nearly shot off, hanging by the skin. "I began to scold the New Mexicans and called them a pack of damned brutes and cowards," White wrote.

An old Indian with a bow and arrow stood armed. The Mexicans in the process of reloading, asked White to ask the old Indian to put down his bow and they would let him go.

Said White: "The Indian handed them to me and I shall never forgive myself for having taken the word of those villains, for villains they were, of the blackest kind. As soon as they saw the Indian without arms [bow and arrow], they came near and riddled him with bullets."

White left the New Mexicans and headed toward Taos with his partner. Several days later he camped with some Paiutes when the New Mexicans struck again. This time all but two escaped. They tied up the two captives. White agonized:

"When they were about to shoot the two Indians, I was so indignant that I raised my gun, aimed at one of the gang, and pulled the trigger, and it wouldn't fall...10 or 12 guns were pointed at me, but they said this is what saved me. 'Que! No es pecado mater esos indios gentiles' ('Oh, well. It's no sin to kill those pagan Indians.')."[15]

White's partner begged him to be quiet and White feared for his life until he reached Taos.

White returned to California in 1840 with a party of New Mexican immigrants and American trappers and traders, John Rowland, William Workman, and Ben Wilson to name three. The Mexican Governor granted Miguel Blanco three leagues (9 x 9 miles) of land at the opening of the Cajon Pass, Rancho Muscupiabe. He was to keep Indian raiders out of the valley, but ironically he lost his own stock to raiding Utes and New Mexicans. White gave up his grant in frustration. White did, however, obtain his property back and more after Americans took over California and he won a law suit.[16]

Underneath all these overt records, one must assume that much unrecorded covert slave activity took place and that the slave business continued after the United States legally became masters of the Southwest in 1848.

California and Nevada Tribes.

American Take Over

Americans in California stood second to none in using the labors of others for their own benefit. Americans occupied both New Mexico and California in 1846, consummating the takeover with the Treaty of Guadalupe Hidalgo in 1848. Immediately laws regarding Native Americans in California were harsh and unfair. Some aspects are as follows:[1]

1. Justices of the Peace shall have jurisdiction in all cases of complaints by, for, or against Indians in their respective townships in this state.

2. Persons and proprietors of land on which Indians are residing shall permit such Indians peaceably to reside on such lands, unmolested in the pursuit of their usual avocations for the maintenance of themselves and families, etc.

3. Any person having, or hereafter obtaining a minor Indian, male or female, from the parent or relations of such Indian minor, and wishing to keep it, such person shall go before a Justice of the Peace, in his township, (who) shall give such person a certificate, authorizing him or her to have the care, custody, control and earnings of such a minor, until he or she obtain the age of majority.

Sections 14 and 20 provided that Indian criminals may be fined and be forced to work out their sentence. Indians caught "loitering and strolling about," frequenting places where liquors are sold, begging, or leading immoral lives may be placed in someone's custody, not to exceed four months.

These vague phrases, with the explicit double standards of value, had the desired effect. Major Horace Bell stated that Los Angeles had its slave mart, as well as New Orleans and Constantinople, only slaves at Los Angeles were sold 52 times a year as long as they lived. The practice at Los Angeles was to gather up all the Indian drunks during Saturday and Sunday and sell them on Monday morning to the ranchers, who then worked them until Friday and paid them in liquors. Consequently they became intoxicated again and were herded into a corral where they could be sold on Monday.[2]

According to Chemehuevi Tribal Leader Charles Wood, Los Angeles County passed an ordinance in 1860 that allowed this auctioning of southland Indians. The life of the Indian under such conditions was extremely short. The San Francisco *Daily Morning Call* on November 24, 1858, related that the same system occurred throughout the state. When the "Digger" in Fresno became drunk and had no money to pay his fine, he was sold at auction to the highest bidder. The editor of the Mariposa *Star* saw one Indian resold for $1.25.[3]

In north-central California "Whole villages of Miwok Indians just disappeared," said Rick Adams, a Maidu Indian at the Maidu Interpretive Center in Roseville while relating stories about his great grandmother Peméla Cleanso (1834-1934) and his Maidu ancestors. Most Indians in the Sacramento area were affluent; they had plenty of great weather, water, seeds, game, fish, birds, acorns, berries, and especially salmon. After Americans took over California in 1848, tragedy took these people. Almost 3000 disappeared! Just disappeared, according to Adams' grand parents. Indians were rounded up, herded into corrals and forced to the central valley. White men took children away from families. Peméla Cleanso, however, was allowed to keep her children because her father John Kapu was a Hawaiian Kanaka, one of ten Kanakas brought to California by John Sutter in 1839. Thus her children of mixed blood could stay with her. Paméla and her children survived, and later she had two other Hawaiian fishermen husbands. Richard Burrill in his book *River of Sorrows* included a painting of the "Maidu Walk." Of 461 Maidu who started this forced march of 125 miles from Chico to the Round Valley Reservation, only 277 reached Round Valley. That is a 25 percent death rate!It was a California "Trail of Tears."[4] Ironically they marched past their sacred mountains Sutter Buttes, the mountains that permeated their physical and spiritual lives.

It is quite true that other factors caused the disappearance of numerous California Indians. Anthropologist Jack Forbes quoted Mariana Vallejo that small pox hit northern California from Ft. Ross to Sonoma, killing 70,000 Indians—though probably quite exaggerated, the numbers appal modern readers. Also from 1830-33, one-half of the Indian population of the Sacramento Valley supposedly was wiped out because of malaria introduced from the north, attributed to John Work and trappers from Hudson Bay Company. But Forbes also asserted that 5,000 Indians were captured from the interior of California and taken to the missions. After secularization in 1833-4, neophytes were not needed in the missions but were wanted more for labor.[5] Instead of mission land being turned over to Indians, it was granted to Californians, and the Indians were at the mercy of these new owners or off on their own to survive.

Under the 1850 California law "for the Government and Protection of Indians," the incongruous and ironic title of the law juxtaposes with the meanings of the law: any white citizen could indenture the labor of an Indian child if he could prove to a judge that the child was an orphan, taken in good conscience. The worst that could happen to someone who failed to feed, clothe, and treat the child humanely was a $10 fine and the reassignment to another master. The law condoned the kidnapping and sale of women and children for household labor.[6]

A few Californians protested these abusive laws that were revised almost yearly from 1850-1870. The editor of *Daily Alta California* in 1853 pleaded that the legislature not pass this year's revision, the "new bill the purport of which was to reduce the Indians to a state of slavery." Indians could be apprenticed to white people similar to the Mormon bill of 1853 [see Chapter 9], but the intent in California was to exploit Indian labor, "to render the miserable degraded remnants of a happy race... [to make them] servants and dependents of their exterminators."[7]

The bill passed: a white man could not be convicted on the testimony of an Indian; an Indian could not give testimony either for or against a white man, a judge could determine justice for or against an Indian (Although the state lifted this restriction against Negroes in 1863, the state kept it for Native Americans.); punishment for vagrancy law violators could be meted out for 12 months for the Indian "to behave himself" or "to betake to some honest employment for support"; he could be hired out to the highest bidder; even in 1855 "greasers," mixed issue of Mexican and Indian, had similar prejudicial restrictions.[8]

Early California traveler William Brewer commented about Indian treatment in California in the 1860s: "It has been a regular business to steal Indian children and bring them down to the civilized parts of the state, even to San Francisco and sell them—not as slaves, but as servants to be kept as long as possible. Mendocino County had been the scene of many of these stealings, and it is said that some of the kidnappers would often get consent of the parents by shooting prevent opposition." The poignant sarcasm pointed out the horrendous tragedies that happened to these unfortunate Native Americans in California.[9]

During the early American occupation of the Napa region, pioneer settler F. A. Van Winkle said she bought "one Indian girl from a Spaniard for $100, but soon after that another Indian girl and two boys came to my house of their own accord and explained that they had no home and wanted to work. The four of them did all my work, washing, ironing, cooking and housecleaning. One of the girls was a splendid nurse. The shameful treatment of the Indians by the Spanish was never equaled by the whites [This is certainly a debatable statement.]. As Americans settled the country the enslaving of young Indians naturally stopped."[10] She said that "All the Spanish families had Indian slaves. They never permitted them to walk, but made them go about on the trot all the time. These Indians made good slaves, excellent. The Spanish vaqueros used to go up to what is now Ukiah and ride in among the Indian rancherias and drive out the boys and girls, leaving mothers behind and killing the bucks if they offered any resistance. Then they would herd the captives down like so many cattle and sell them to the ranchers. About $100 was the standard price. A good girl would bring that, but some sold for as little as $50."

Trapper George C. Yount, a neighbor of Van Winkle and famous trapper who settled in the Napa region in the 1840s, stated that Napa Valley had about 8,000 humans (Indians) and within a few years they were reduced to hundreds.[11]

Indians attempted to protect themselves, to retaliate for wrongs done to them, and to survive after land and food sources were taken from them. But then the retaliation against these attempts to defend themselves and their rights harmed Indians even more.

The United States government tried to protect Indians from the aggression, abuse and exploitation by the whites. To help the Indians, the government needed to give them land with enough resources to sustain themselves, to remove them from roads used by Americans, to help Natives with farm and animal resources, and to keep them from valuable lands that the whites coveted.

California and the Federal government initiated a reservation and Indian farm system. It, no doubt, saved hundreds of lives. Though well-meaning people and officials tried conscientiously to help, a decade of chaos existed during the 1850s and into the 1860s. These basic goals generally failed because of civilizations pushing almost everywhere, greed and appetite for land by whites, political pressure to keep the government from giving away public land, and lack of money to fund plans adequately.

Failure to implement these meager attempts came also as a result of inexperience in establishing California Indian farms and reservations, distance from Washington, D.C., poor management and inefficiency, changes of superintendents every time the Democrats or Whigs lost the presidency, corruption of superintendents and Indian agents, and finally the vicissitudes of farming and ranching (rust wiping out wheat crops, cattle destroying crops and orchards, periodic droughts occurring in the 1850s and 1860s). Traders hurt or helped morale—depending on one's point of view--by selling liquor to Indians and by Indians being adept at sneaking liquor into the reservations.

Officials assigned to help Indians sometimes took advantage of Native Americans or of the position assigned to these officials. Indian Agent Lt. E. E. Beale at Ft. Tejon, ended up owning most of the Indian land of which he was in charge. He made a claim on 22 leagues of the Spanish land grant that the Sebastian Reservation was on and ended up owning 87,750 acres.[2] "This is the way to get land," Brewer sarcastically said. It was also suspicious that cattle for Indians ended up on officials' ranches throughout California, including that of Sam Bishop, the one the town of Bishop was named after.

Bonnie Ketterl Kane's book *A View from the Ridge Route* beautifully documented the chaos of one reservation's attempts to protect southern California Indians at Ft. Tejon Reservation, officially called Sebastian Indian Reservation.[3] She described how Lt. Beale (later made a general) ended up owning Rancho La Liebre for three cents an acre, deeded in the name of Mary E. Beale. The rancho had been part of the Sebastian Reservation that was reduced from 763,000 acres in Col. Barbour's treaty of 1851 to 150,000 and finally to 75,000 acres in 1853. These acres were part of the "Lost Land" when the U.S. Senate refused to ratify the treaty with 119 bands of California Indians [see "Lost Land" below].

Then a few years later, besides his first estate Rancho La Liebre, Beale owned Ft. Tejon itself and charged $1,000 a year for 1,200 acres of land to allow a couple hundred Indians to stay on the land that was developed by Indian labor and government money. Beale owned buildings built with adobe bricks made by Indians. He was generous enough to reduce it $200 per year from his asking rental price of $1,200 a year. That was a good amount of money in the 1860s.

Tejon's Agent Col. James R. Vineyard in 1856 reportedly owned several thousand sheep on the reservation, herded by Indians. He later retired in the area. According to the 1860 census James Vineyard owned property and livestock worth $45,000--a tidy sum in 1860. Kane also stated that some reservation employees claimed reservation land and used Indians to develop that land.[14]

Supplies purchased by government money for Indians quite often ended in white men's hands, and stock was often sold to whites. Indians took care of animals belonging to Beale and Bishop and the old trapper Alex Goday. Supposedly cattle for Indians were driven up Owens Valley (where the town of Bishop was established) and sold to miners. The author heard some 35 years ago that Beale, Bishop and Goday were involved in diverting Indian cattle to the mining areas of Owens Valley, but possesses no documentation on this.

Government negotiators made a treaty with the California Cahuilla, Serrano, Los Coyotes, and Cupaños tribes that gave them thousands of acres where I-15 runs today from San Bernardino County to San Diego County—enough land to survive and prosper. The treaty was signed in southern California and peace followed. President Millard Fillmore recommended this omnibus bill be passed by the Senate allocating 7,500,000 acres of California land to the 119 groups of California Indians. But the Senate never ratified it.[15] The so called "lost land" disappeared from the records in 1852, only to reappear in 1905, 53 years later!

California's legislature had a part in the bill's defeat. It sent these instructions with their senators: "Resolved, that our Senators in Congress be instructed to oppose the confirmation of any and all treaties with Indians of the State of California, granting to Indians an exclusive right to occupy any of the public lands of the state." What the Senate allocated was less than 10 percent of the treaty land-- a mere 517,000 acres for the 119 Indian tribes. In fact, in another request the State asked to "remove bodily" all Indians from the state. That fortunately the Senate did not agree to do.[16]

The Moapa Reservation for Paiutes in Nevada suffered the same fate. It had one million acres allocated to it, 20 miles long. When the agreement came back from Washington, the Moapa reservation too had been stripped of the bulk of their treaty land, receiving only 1,000 acres.[17]

Both the 1851 and 1852 Annual Reports of the U. S. Commissioner of Indian Affairs bragged that the government signed over 50 treaties allocating land for Indian reservations and that 174 million acres had been ceded to the United States by Indians. Both Commissioners were not sure how many treaties the Senate would sign. Both also had disturbing words about the outlook for Indians. One said in 1851 that the job dealing with Indians was "hopeless and helpless." He wished Superintendent for Indian Affairs in New Mexico James S. Calhoun, who was also the governor, would be more of a superintendent than just in name. The very religious Commissioner George W. Manypenny lamented in 1852 that Americans moved west for good new land and ignored right of Indians. He pled for "humanity, Christianity, and national honor" because America needed laws to protect Indians. However, treaties the Senate signed received Indian land signed over to the United States, but Indians in California only received a small portion of their treaty land.[18] Commissioner Charles E. Mix reported that California had 11,239 Indians located on reservations with an annual budget of $1,173,000; Oregon had 3,200 Indians in two reservations; Texas only 1,483; New Mexico 212,506; Utah 172,000.

William P. Dole, Commissioner from 1861-63, complained about California "indentured" laws which was just another name for "enslaving." The so called "Indian War," he said, was only a white war. Indians were "hunted down like beasts, murdered and kidnapped." Dole in 1863 praised Utes for signing treaties but knew they were not about to settle down. He lavished praise on the Pueblos in New Mexico as "unwavering in their loyalty and devotion to the government." Pueblos were of great service in protecting the frontiers. Still, he said, Indians were stealing thousands of sheep, cattle, horses, and there was much "suffering of others who have been carried into captivity." He said California needed to eliminated some reservation so that Indian were "unmolested by whites." Miners "despoil their homes, the graves of their ancestors, and the means of supplying their rude and simple wants."

Another Commissioner, N. G. Taylor, pleading with President Andrew Johnson in 1868 that he did not want the military to be in charge of Indian affairs, because for 17 years the army had unfortunate results, like starving the Navajos and committing indiscretions. He said it would be better, more humane to poison Indians with big fiestas and cooked beef with "wolf bane" (poison). That would be better than the slow death with Indians "lingering [with] syphililic [sic] poisons" around military posts.[19]

Even Indian workers that got along with whites in Southern California did not have the ideal work conditions. John P. Sherburne, who observed Indians in the San Bernardino area while with Lt. A. Whipple in 1854, affirmed, "The Indian laborers were domesticated Cahuillas, both artist Mollhausen and Whipple commented on the malnourished appearance and lowly status as peons of the estate."[20]

The decade of the 1850s was disastrous to the California Indian. It displaced Indians and bands and poor and hungry people. Indians stole cattle and horses, killing them by the hundreds over the years. A few Indians attacked and killed white people around the state—some of whom committed atrocities that warranted punishment. But to raid a rancheria and kill over 20 men, women and children as punishment for the loss of a few cows was out-of-proportion retribution.

Editors of the book *Exterminate Them* found several hundred letters and newspapers accounts replete with ruthless incidents of California savagery toward Native Californians. Vociferous demands of a minority of Californians was just short of calls for genocide. Although a few newspapers were appalled at the treatment of Indians, most printed bias, sometimes exaggerated claims of Indian violations that spurred further aggression toward Indians. Here are samples of Californian overkill incidents:[21]

> June 1853--"and six of them were shot down" (in a white man's camp).
> June 1853--Capt. H. W. Wessels reported a "barbarously" murder of "inoffensive Indian" by "one of a class of lawless ruffians whose wanton aggressions upon the Indians"—the murderer escaped.
> Aug. 1859--"succeeds in killing ten Indians including one squaw."

June 1860—"one of our informants saw twenty-six bodies of women and children some infants at the breast... [whose] whole numbers slaughtered in a single night was two hundred and forty."

Dec. 1859—"attacking the enemy succeeded in killing 32 and taking two prisoners."

March 1853—"rocks rolled into the cave, and the wretched inmates, rushing out for safety, met danger a thousand times more dreadful shot by Capt. Geo Rose thirteen killed . Three women and five children were spared...Capt. Rose took one child, Mr. Lattimer another and the others (divided among the party).

Nov. 1851—"few prisoners will be taken."

June 1849—"separated men from women and children...men broke and attempted to escape...fourteen...were slaughtered on the spot...white men took a small party of women and children prisoners...killed 20...22 men and thirty-four women and children are yet missing from the rancheria."

Paraphrased: Said a Mexican horse trader in northern California: "I'll give you three horses for each Indian woman you get." When they met again, the Californian had about 90 horses for his ranch--

June 1860—"The butchery was confined to women and children [Digger tribes], the men being absent at the time."

Feb. 1857--"killed ten wounded forty."

March 1853—"An Indian was captured and shot through the head for stealing, another was hung at Reading's ranch."[22]

The great Indian land of plenty in California where for thousands of years idyllic life was the general manner of living had come to an end. These small independent units of 50-300 people lost their independence, one by one, just short of genocide. Dreams for their children and grandchildren ended in displacement, death, or servitude. Choose any Indian metaphor--it doesn't matter: the Great Spirit was lost, the "right path" was blocked, the individual's "song" was gone, the beloved land where ancestors slept disappeared, and everything they loved "was gone the way of the earth."

Californians exploited other minorities too. The Chinese women were used in a somewhat different way except they were not transported over the Mojave Trail. On December 10, 1858, the *Daily Morning Call* had two articles exposing the ways in which the Chinese women were obtained for individual use--to offset the woman shortage in the unsettled mining period. Conspirators laid false charges against a Chinese husband to get him away from his wife. When he was released after a day or so, his wife had already been abducted. A wealthy and clever citizen of Mariposa had the court award him custody of a Chinese lady until she worked off her debt to him.[23] Although the editor of the *Daily Morning Call* and others frowned upon this type of activity, it was several years before it subsided and California became tame.

Non-corrupt government people who truly cared were powerless to help much. Chaotic and corrupt reservations and farm systems helped little. Helplessness permeated California in the 10-15 years after the Gold Rush. The rest of the Old Southwest gradually eliminated slavery.

When Americans took charge of New Mexico, slavery decreased and church baptism records showed the drop over the years, finally showing a decrease in "Ute" baptisms according to Warren:[24] In the 1840s New Mexicans baptized 157 "Utes," but only 26 in the 1860s and one in the 1870s; the Paiutes were baptized as follows: 7 in the 1830s, 44 in the 1840s, 18 in the 1850s, 15 in the 1860s and only one in the 1870s. Yet Indian slavery was still not over.

Slavery residue existed all over the Southwest. Little incidents surfaced in various parts of the west. On the upper end of the Arkansas River, for example, an American soldier shuttered in Bent's Fort when a group of Cheyenne came into the fort to secure a doctor's help for a sick emaciated girl covered with sores. She was a captive purchased from the Kiowas. "Unable to walk she subsisted on tuna [fruit] plucked from the prickly pear through which she had been dragged by a pony harnessed between two poles upon the rear of which a basket-like litter had been woven."[25] The doctor noted she might not live long. But she did. After camp women bathed her, fed and clothed her, she improved in a few days. One little girl saved from servitude in the west.

Finally Slavery Ends

Some Americans attempted to stop abuses toward Indians. James S. Calhoun, both Indian agent for Santa Fe and also governor of the territory of New Mexico, recommended in early 1850s congressional action[1] to stop the slave trade. Congress, however, had more urgent concerns: the Fugitive Slave Law, Kansas-Nebraska Act, and looming fears of the country dividing over the Negro slavery issue.

Mormons tried to curtail New Mexican slavers and horse-riding Utes from their slaving activities in Utah Territory. Mormons were appalled at the Indian purchases "from time immemorial." Utah Territorial Governor Brigham Young and the Latter Day Saints church felt obligated to stop Indian slavery. It was "Our duty towards them upon the common principles of humanity." Utah settlers abhorred that Indians even gambled their own children and those captured by war or theft. Some children were "lariatted out to subsist upon grass and roots or starve." If the Indians became troublesome to the raiders, they were frequently killed.[2] One story is told about a Ute chief tying three children to a bush, letting them eat grass voraciously while he negotiated their price.

Later Day Saint officials brought New Mexican citizen Pedro León Lújan and his traders before a Mormon judge for slave trading.[3] He had been given a trading permit by governor James S. Calhoun but not for buying slaves. His defense was that Paiutes had stolen many of their horses, had killed them, and had eaten some. Indians gave eight children (five boys and three girls) and one woman to León's group in compensation for the lost horses. Well, León got caught with all those Indian children. The judges denied the defense and freed the eight children and one woman.[4] In a letter from León's Santa Fe friend and former Indian agent for Abiquiu Lafayette Head in "regards to the buying and selling of Payutahs" on April 30, 1852:

"Pedro León left Abiquiu to trade with Indians at Salt Lake. The Indians stole his animal he applied to authorities at Salt Lake and recovered them—He was taken to the jail and confined for six weeks but was treated well.

"He has the whole proceedings of the trail.

"He contends he has the right by custom to trade for the Payutah children—He gave the parents horses which were killed for food—The parents gave the children but not for slaves—they are adopted into the [and he added "trusted"]family of those who get them are baptized and remain as one of the family—The head of the house standing as God-father The Prefect has a right to free them whenever maltreated The Indian has a right to choose a guardian—

"Women are freed whenever married say from 14 to 16

"Men ditto from 18 to 20—at the death of Godfather never sold always freed

"The Godfathers provide husbands & wives for them the same as their own children—When the Godfather dies they are free—As soon as they are baptized they can't be sold any more than the Mexican children—It would be contrary to the laws of the Church—They are not Peons-they have no debts to work out
They first learn to talk then the Lord's Prayer then Baptized & adopted.
"There is no Mexican law on the subject only custom.
"They eat snakes toads lyands [lizards] worms grasshoppers
"Who can tell the Boundry lines of New Mexico[?]"

In the Appendix of *Indian Slave Trade in the Southwest,* author Bailey cited, "An Act for the Relief of Indian Slaves and Prisoners," an attempt by Governor Brigham Young and the territorial legislature of Utah to stop slavery. Slavery had been so prevalent in Utah that the "Indians consider it allowable traffic and frequently offer their prisoners or children for sale."[5] The Mormon plan was to release them from slavery by buying them and binding them to some avocation,that is, teaching them a white man's job. They were to be indentured to a "master," usually a Mormon family, who would provide Indian children from ages seven to 16 schooling for three months a year if a school were in their district and clothe them appropriate to the master's lifestyle. The judge determined the length of service, never to exceed 20 years. Mormons therefore purchased slaves "out of slavery."

Two forces then curtailed New Mexican slavery, the effort of Mormons to keep peace with Indians in Utah Territory and determination to stop Ute Indians and New Mexicans from capturing slaves. Also there was a general determination of American settlers in California and New Mexico to stand against slavery *per se*. California voted to be a free state in their Constitution of 1849, i.e., free from Negro slavery. But as already noted, virtual Indian slavery permeated California. New Mexico was allowed to vote for slavery or not because of the popular sovereignty law passed by Congress in the 1850s. But the majority of immigrants coming into New Mexico and California were anti-slavery.

Though New Mexico tried to eliminate the peonage or servitude system, it still persisted. In two divorce cases, for example, in 1861 in Valencia County and 1864 in Bernalillo,[6] two husbands sued for divorce and return of property that belonged to the plaintiff and each had listed an Indian servant as property. In the 1861 case Juan Pablo Apodaca, accusing his wife of leaving his bed and committing adultery, wanted her to return property of ten *fanegas* of wheat, ten *fanegas* of corn and one Indian servant—"all property of the said plaintiff for which he preys judgment." The use of the term "property" for a captive Indian showed vestiges of a lingering slavery system.

Throughout slavery history there were incidents of captives not wanting to be returned. Several English colonists on the East Coast lived with their captors so long that they became, in a sense, Indian. The same occasionally was true of Indians captured by Europeans. A few became attached to the ones who continued to sexually assault them, even becoming part of the family, accepting the slave status and abuse. Perhaps it is like the person who has been in prison so long that that becomes his life.

Captive aborigines often did not wish to be repatriated, ransomed or given back to their natal groups. Josiah Gregg on the Santa Fe Trail offered to buy some Mexican slaves from the Comanche in the late 1830s, and take them back to Matamoros and Chihuahua, Mexico. Only one boy chose to go back. The women and girls decided against being returned to Mexico. One girl, in particular, had been "married." Would she rather live with her new forced-kin or return to her father in Matamoros? Facing this push-pull dilemma, she chose the life of the plains with the Comanche rather than the possible shame, derision, dishonor of her father and the unknown attitude of her Mexican village.

Twenty years earlier, stated Gregg, the Governor-General of Chihuahua, paid $1,000 to a trader to ransom his daughter who had been captured. She sent a note to her father stating she was married and pregnant, disfigured by a Comanche tattoo, and declined to be returned.[7]

Gregg asked one boy, "Are you not a Mexican?" He answered in Spanish, "Bernardino Saenz, sir, at your service." He said that he was once until four years before he had been taken. When Gregg asked Saenz if he wanted to be bought back, the boy answered, "No, señor, I am too much a brute to live among Christians."

One Navajo warrior, formerly a Hopi boy captured by Navajos, twice warned Oraibi villagers of the pending onslaughts of a huge Navajo raiding party. He tried to save Hopi lives. He rode close to the Hopi defense, saying, "Do not try to defend the whole mesa. There are too many of us. Defend the village instead....I am *Nuvakwahu*, Snow Eagle. I was born a Hopi in Oraibi, but I was stolen by the Navajos when I was small. Now I also am a Navajo."[8]

Again he tried to help but was killed in the last part in the bloody raid against his former relatives. When his body was found, his grandmother claimed him and his former people gave him a Hopi burial. He helped save Oraibi from capture. Though he became a Navajo, it seems as if one never forgets, never loses all his natal life; he still had attachments and loyalties.

When President Andrew Johnson tried to help New Mexican Indian captives return to their people in the late 1860s, dozens did not wish to be repatriated. Many peons lived their lives out by choice with their New Mexican families.

For years after the Treaty of Guadalupe Hildalgo in 1848, hundreds were in various forms of servitude. For example, when Lt. A. Whipple was in New Mexico in 1853 preparing for his Federal railroad survey across the 35th parallel, he almost lost his hired muleteer in Laguna, New Mexico:

Whipple saved a Mexican muleteer named Torrivio from being sent back to a life of servitude. Torrivio was once a peon who had run away. His previous owner in Laguna tried to reclaim him, wherein a fight ensued. Whipple intervened and advanced Torrivio some wages--fifteen dollars placated the owner and kept Torrivio from being bound for life.[9]

Sadly Whipple lost muleteer Torrivio. When the exploring trip was just over 100 miles from completion at Afton Canyon on the Mojave

River, Torrivio remained behind the expedition to bring up two tired mules. Paiutes (perhaps Chemeheuvis) had been lurking around the hills and took advantage of the lone and unarmed man. When Torrivio did not come back to camp, Whipple sent two groups back to find either him or his body. One patrol found his arrow-ridden and blood-matted clothes in a Paiute camp where a mule had been cooked. The Indians escaped but the patrol destroyed everything of value in the camp.[10]

Even the two Mojave guides had been wary of the Paiute and had expected an attack two days before. When the Mojave Indian guides reached Punta del Agua by present Minneola Road (Yermo), they refused the offer of two mules because they had to return to their village through the hostile Paiute.[11] These Paiutes by the 1850s had been mixed with mission runaways, secularized mission Indians or escapees from southern California ranchos. These Indians changed the nature and disposition of the usually docile Paiute Indians on the Mojave Desert.

The Mojave Trail, like the rest of California, also took awhile to settle down. The later trading activity on the Mojave Trail was slightly reversed. The Paiutes did some raiding on their own. They stole horses and supplies from desert travelers and extracted a little tribute from travelers crossing their territories:[12] a couple cows here, a worn out horse there, or a bucket of hasty pudding (mixed flour and water). Though Old Spanish Trail merchants probably had to pay a tribute for safe passage through some Indian groups, not enough journals were written to prove the traders had many problems.

In the early 1860s native desert Indians aggressively attacked travelers and early ranches in the desert. On the former Old Spanish Trail, on the Mojave River, a few miles southwest of Barstow at Cottonwood, Indians killed Robert Wilburn who was following tracks of Indians that stole stock he was looking after. When he disappeared, searchers found him pierced with three arrows. They blamed Paiutes, but it could have been Chemehuevi or renegade Indians.

In another attack at Bitter Spring, an isolated waterhole on the now Los Angeles-Salt Lake Road, Indians met a freighting party of 14 wagons before they reached Bitter Springs coming from Utah, saying they knew where there was better pasturage near the springs. Jehed Jackman and Thomas Williams, brothers-in-law, agreed to travel with the Indians to see the site. Williams trusted Paiutes; in fact, he and his wife raised a Paiute baby found in a cradleboard after a battle. The grass was better, but as the two traders headed back to bring the wagons to the grass, they were hit with a volley of arrows. Jackman fell from his horse, hit by seven arrows, two passing through his body. Williams made it back to the wagons but soon died. Freighters buried Williams and found Jackman still alive. They took him to Aaron Lane's ranch at Oro Grande crossing of the Mojave River. Williams lingered for a month before dying in San Bernardino.

California authorities sent Major James Carleton from Ft. Tejon to chastise Indians. He did. Any Indians. He scoured desert waterholes from Las Vegas to the San Bernardino Mountains. His policy was to keep Indians away from the waterholes to make sure they did not harm any more whites. He executed five and left two of them hanging near Williams' grave. He severed the heads of the others and placed the impaled heads at Bitter Springs and another Indian site.

Indians stayed away from army units. Carleton released a captive woman and sent her back to her rancheria to ask the chiefs to have peaceful talks. Indians came from as far away as Las Vegas. They agreed to leave the whites alone if the army would not molest the Indians.

A few other attacks occurred in Summit Valley where Indians killed three cattlemen and at Salt Springs Mine where they caused the death of five miners—both incidents on the Mojave River Trail. Though Carleton was praised by some, he was greatly criticized for his ruthlessness.[13]

A little later the army established Camp Cady east of Yermo on the Mojave Road to supply Camp Mojave on the Colorado River and to deter Indian attacks on travelers. Camp Cady was about 30 miles south of Bitter Spring.[14]

The U.S. Government finally thought they had solved the problems of Indian raids, i.e., against Indians and by Indians: they removed them from the immigrant routes and also helped pioneers by stopping Indian tribute requests. The army put Indians on reservations in the 1860s and 1870s.

In an under-estimation, New Mexicans and people of Arizona in1866 held 2,000 Apaches. That was 20 years after American rule started in 1846. An American officer said Apaches begged him to help recover 29 children stolen by Arizona citizens. The spokesman said, "...our little boys will grow up as slaves, and our girls will be diseased prostitutes...."[15]

In 1868 someone asked Navajo Chief Barboncito in New Mexico how many of his group were missing and held captive somewhere. His startling answer was, "Over half the tribe"[16]

Martha Blue in her book about Indian Trader J. L. Hubbell stated that businessmen like Indian trading posts profited from the lucrative trading in slaves. Blue estimated: "Between 1700 and 1870, some 1600 Navajos (mostly women, who were prized for their weaving skills, and children) entered Hispanic households as slaves.[17] Most of these women or their off springs eventually became integrated with the New Mexican culture.

But even then there were questionable incidents which may bring into focus a type of slavery on the ranches and gold and silver mines of the desert. One incident was penned in 1867 in William Jackson's diary.

Young Jackson, traveling the Mojave Trail from Utah, narrated that near the present Oro Grande on the Mojave River, a rancher had several captive Indian women, one of whom was locked up in his outhouse. The circumstances and motives behind the rancher's actions lead to interesting speculation. But it must be assumed the woman was not in there on her own volition. Perhaps the early desert rancher topped the Mojave and the Mexicans both in inventing a new twist to the inhuman institution of slavery.[18] More investigation is needed to bring light to the intricacies of this and other forms of human bondage in America's west.

Despite the Treaty of Guadalupe Hidalgo in 1848 stating the two countries should help stop slave stealing over the border, Comanche and Apache continued sporadic raids into Mexico. In California Vincente P. Gomez wrote his memoirs in 1876, one part of which was entitled *"Venta de ninos indios en los Angeles"* (selling Indian children in Los Angeles) about a trader in 1857 using the alias Don Francisco Castillo buying young Indians from Lower California and selling them in Los Angeles. It was not certain whether Castillo purchased "inditos" from their own bands or whether he purchased them from other preying Indians as New Mexicans had purchased Paiutes from the Utes and Navajos. What was certain was that he used subterfuge in his frequent trips to the mountains of Lower California, always with *"...con objecto de comprar inditos p. venderlos en Los Angeles"* (object of buying Indian youngsters to sell in Los Angeles).[19]

From the sparse documents like the above in Spanish, New Mexico, Utah and California archives, historians can only learn a minute part of what happened in the interior areas of California, of the New Mexican frontier north of Abiquiu, and along the 1200-miles journey from New Mexico to California and back, i.e., the Old Spanish Trail. Luckily for historians, a few facts and incidents have been found, analyzed and written as partial histories. At least those interested in America's past have something, and they can conjecture about dramas that took place in the vast west during the 18th and 19th centuries.

Effects Never Ending

Effects of the Southwest slavery were never ending. Even though participants in 19th century enslavement, perpetrators and victims alike, those killed in slave raiding and those enslaved, all have "gone the way of the earth" as stated in 1946 by author William R. Palmer, an adopted Paiute, effects of slavery continued. Like the scars of old Indian trails and campsites on the desert floor, signs of Indian slavery remain.

Slavery changed genetic pools of New Mexicans and Californios, with millions of people having Indian blood all over the west. Breakdown of bands and tribes of Indians caused some to become extinct or to move in with other villages or pueblos. Slave dealing made Indian tribes more diverse.

Even traditional enemies like the Ute and Navajos changed. At the turn of the century around 1900, a Navajo translator Clah-chris-chili (Left-Handed Curley Man) was a tribal judge. Clah's father years before went to Utah and bought three Ute girls for three blankets. He brought them back to Teec-nos-pos, married two of them, and gave one to his brother. Navajo men traditionally did not marry a Ute, but Ute captive girls from raiding parties might marry a Navajo when she reached adolescence. Clah was a product of the Navajo-Ute marriage, a descendent from a Ute slave.[1]

Living into the 20th century near Cedar City, Utah, was Paiute Jinnie Curley Jim. Navajos captured this Paiute when she was a child, but she "found her way back to her people after long years of servitude and exile."[2]

Joseph Toulouse, Jr. found old colonial blankets in 1959 in the mountain village of Abo Viejo in the Manzano Mountains, 70 miles southeast of Albuquerque. He was told about even more beautiful blankets in a remote village of Punta de Agua belonging to Manuelita Otero. When Toulouse visited Senora Otero, he saw what Toulouse called a Navajo "Slave Blanket," and was told a remarkable story that transcends the chronology of New Mexican history.

The first generation of Otero weavers began with a Navajo slave girl named Guadalupe Salaz who was taken prisoner in the 1860s Navajo Wars. Guadalupe escaped from the Navajo prisoner area of Bosque Redondo but was captured by a party of Mexicans gathering salt and then held as a slave by a Señor Otero, the leader of the group. The pretty Navajo girl married the oldest Otero son and soon Manuelita Otero was born. The weaving tradition continued by the Otero family into the late 20th century, the sixth generation in 1959. The family still had possession of two rugs done by Guadalupe, in the Navajo style on a Navajo loom, not a Spanish loom. The Navajo bloodline of this slave girl continues in New Mexico today.[3]

After the Mojave turned 16-year-old slave Olive Oatman over to the military at Ft. Yuma, Olive became a celebrity. Anthropologist A. L. Kroeber said there is not enough known about Olive's adult life to be able to judge the effect of her captivity on her adult happiness. The state legislature of California appropriated $1,500 for her to get her started in a new life. She never received it and no one knows where the money went. She boarded a ship in San Pedro to stay with relatives in Oregon. On the way she met Rev. Royal B. Stratton of Yreka, California, who convinced her to tell her story in a book that he would write. The book sold 30,000 copies in 1857 and went through several editions.

Just before the Civil War she visited a Mojave friend, Beautiful Bird, and Olive said, "We met as friends, giving the left hand in friendship," which is held as a sacred pledge among several tribes. Soon after she married John Brand Fairchild, she stopped her public speaking and wore a dark veil to hide her tattooed face. Her husband bought her books and photographs and burned them. In obscurity, she died in Sherman, Texas, in 1903.[4] She was evidently not able to conceive children but she and Fairchild adopted one. Oatman helped in community projects most of her adult life.

A bright spot occurred after years of California reservation mismanagement and greed. Former southern California Indian Superintendent Edward Beale, former hero of the Bear Flag Revolt, chosen to lead the Camel Experiment in 1857, former Surveyor General of California befriended southern California Indians. When Ft. Tejon closed as a military base and as an Indian reservation, Beale allowed local Indians to stay on a rancheria on his property. He paid Indians to work his land and attend his stock. Therefore a number of Indians survived into the 20th century. Maybe he made amends for suspect actions and accusations during and after the early reservation period. Beale, according to a contemporary Bakersfield resident, exercized a fatherly care over these Indians, allowing them to farm, paying them liberally for their services, and building a chapel for them to worship. When General Beale died, his son Truxtun Beale continued the beneolent policy, allowing the Indians free run of the ranch--"free of rent or any tax." [5]

Slave-trade depopulation had disastrous effect on Paiutes in southern Utah and Nevada. There just were not enough Paiute women left in the little family units. Young boys stolen would not, of course, grow up to help defend their families or mate with the remaining girls. For survival, families had to move away from the route of the Old Spanish Trail or away from roving bands of slave stealers. As groups became weaker, they were more susceptible to raids.

Said Chemehuevi Chairman Charles Wood, "We retreated from known paths and water locations, deeper in the desert in an attempt to protect ourselves."[6]

Three factors affected California Indians. European diseases hurt all Indians in the Americas. Indians had little immunity against measles, chicken pox and small pox. Just like on the East Coast, European contact with coastal tribes spread inland. In the west early Spanish expeditions and settlements after 1769 on the coast spread diseases to the interior valleys killing inland Indians as well as coastal Indians. Spanish explorers and Oñate coming up the Rio Grande in the 1590s also affected Southwest Indians. Add that to the missions constantly needing Indian replenishment, thus raiding for new converts in villages such as Muscupiabit in the Cajon Pass, then over the San Bernardino and San Gabriel Mountains to desert rancherias. Fragile existence became more fragile or non-existent. Finally New Mexican traders and other slavers further decimated Great Basin Indians along the Old Spanish Trail. Groups like the Vanyume in the Mojave Desert were considered extinct. "Vanyume are extinct," said A. L. Kroeber, and their history and relationships to other Indians are "far from clear." [7]

Mission officials or soldiers took two of Donna Yocum's ancestors from their Mojave Desert rancheria in the 1830s and raised and baptized them at San Fernando Mission. Most importantly they survived to produce children, survived mission life and Mexican and American periods after the missions declined. Although Anthropologist A. L. Kroeber listed the Vanyume tribe (band) of Takic speaking Uto-Aztecan

87

language as extinct, Donna Yocum with her mother and her son Chris, now living in Oregon, are Vanyume and are not extinct!

An excavation near a housing development northwest of Victorville in 2004 unearthed a rancheria burial which had two Vanyume remains. From two burials, mitochondrial DNA proved two teeth to be the same DNA as Donna Yocum's and her deceased aunt..[8]

John Valenzuela is also a Vanyume living in Hesperia, California, whose ancestors too survived the experience at San Fernando Mission. He is now Chairman of the San Fernando Band of Mission Indians. Yocum is Vice Chairwoman, Marie Mia is financial secretary, and Melinda Morales was secretary for years (see Appendix A and Appendix B).

So despite European diseases, missions capturing desert Indians, and New Mexican traders killing, capturing and selling them, Vanyumes are still around, over 700 documented Vanyumes survive today.

In places like Las Vegas and Amargosa Valley where there were enough Indians to defend themselves; their population was able to sustain themselves and they moved away, joined other groups, or were placed on reservations. The survivors endured.

Timbisha Indians (Shoshone) around Death Valley also outlasted the odds. Luckily they were just to the north of the Old Spanish Trail. They tolerated the mining period by helping American miners. They survived broken promises of the National Park Service.

Now a little justice occurred. Timbisha Indians received caretaker control over thousand of acres of their ancestral land in California and a little in Nevada. They are now custodians of their ancient homeland. They can camp at their piñon forests in the Panamint Mountains and take care of mesquite trees.[9]

In one long Chemehuevi legend, "How Coyote Went to War Against Gila Monster," Coyote rallies his almost beaten forces to win. One of the losers, however, also illustrates values admired by the Chemehuevi and other Indians: At the end of a losing cause, Turtle turns to face the warriors coming at him and dies with great dignity, thus showing "patience to endure, strength to survive, courage when all hope is lost."[10] Admirable qualities for humans.

Admirable qualities occurred all over the old Southwest. At the turn of the 20th century, new owners of Warner Ranch demanded removal

Precious "artifact in place"--here is an Indian trail 12-15" wide heading toward the Mojave River. Remains of the former Indians using this 4,000-year-old trading corridor, from the coast to the interior deserts. Undoubetedly followed by Vanyume, Mojave and Chemehuevi Indians. Scars on the desert floor reminding us of a varied past. Photo by David Dillon.

Cahuilla Woman, a photo from the Forbes Collection, courtesy of Los Angeles County Museum. The Cahuilla living in Riverside and San Bernardino counties survived the mission period and being in the south avoided the tragedy of the Gold Rush.

of the Cupeño and mixed Indians who lived in this Cupeño area in north San Diego County. Despite vigorous protests by appeals and legal battles, the Cupeño lost and consequently the U. S. Government moved the Cupeño from Kupa to Pala and had "given" them new home sites in Pala, a Luiseño reservation.

Government officials sent children away to school—almost like Oñate did in 1598. Small children went to St. Boniface in Banning and the older children went to Sherman Indian School in Riverside. One can not image the trauma of being forced from one's home of maybe 50 generations of ancestors, and at the same time having one's children taken away.

The elders in 1903, however, according to Cupeño Elder Dadeane Nelson in 2003, showed their character by telling the children the following: "Go, children, go forward in a changing world, study, learn so that you can become a doctor, teacher, lawyer, and one day even a chief. Help yourself and your people, but always remember who you are and be proud." Again, these are great values for all Americans.[11]

The tradition of the "Trade Fairs" that were held in Taos, Santa Fe and Jemez and other frontier towns still continue. In August 2008, for example, millions of dollars of Indian arts and crafts sold to thousands of people and companies in the Indian Market held in Santa Fe . Hundreds of vendors and exhibiters from Indian groups all over the United States vie yearly to be accepted to display their pottery, beads, paintings, baskets and sculptures.[12]

Spanish or Mexican officials regulated (somewhat) the ancient fairs. Now the Southwestern Association for Indian Arts, Inc. (SWAIA) screens and selects Indian artists for authenticity and skill. Acoma, Zuni, Apache, Ute, Navajo, Kiowa, Comanche and dozens of others set up to sell their wares. Purchases go to museums, corporate collections and private collectors. It is a "juried" show, filled with cultural and artistic competition, but not one Indian woman is sold; there are no groups of Indian children, tethered by some grass, waiting to be purchased as slaves, wives, domestics or peons.

But as one looks at the faces of the venders and the buyers, one cannot help but wonder about the backgrounds and the mixed characteristics of these beautiful and peaceful Indians of the Southwest, some descendents of over 200 years of slavery exploitation and of those who survived a raw history.

Another effect is the thousands of documents hidden in the recesses of various museums, historic societies and archives. Below is just one of these records that was uncovered several years ago:

In the Los Angeles Plaza Church death records of 1845, there's a lonely, pathetic entry, just a few words in Spanish, part of an official list recording local deaths. This notation is that of an Indian boy, age unknown, but probably about three years old or less. The boy's name was Santiago. Several years before in the fall, New Mexican traders left Abiquiu, New Mexico, heading to Los Angeles to trade their blankets and other woolen goods. They caught one skinny and undernourished Paiute Indian girl somewhere in the Mojave Desert.

With California winter rains, came grasses in the spring, and caravans rendezvoused near the Cajon Pass and Horsethief Canyon and joined trading parties from the San Diego and northern California. They organized the trip back to New Mexico, loaded with coveted California mules, hundreds of horses, and a dozen or so sheep for food on the two months journey back to Abiquiu.

They left behind the little Indian girl taken from the desert, now baptized in a strange language and named Maria de la Luz. She was probably sold to a rancho owner in the Los Angeles area to become a household servant for the rest of her life. For her Mexican traders received perhaps two mares or one big California mule. The terse and unemotional record under "Deaths" in the Los Angeles Plaza Church is as follows:[13]

"1845 Santiago, Indian child of Maria de la Luz, Indian from New Mexico."

End of Slave Trade book—no, it really isn't the end of slave trade stories.

Appendix A

Vanyume and Kitanemuk Are Not Extinct

As noted in this book, Uto-Aztecan speakers have been in the Mojave Desert and the Great Basin for about 5,000 years. They survived and expanded. Despite 18 and 19th century three misfortunes: (1) European diseases spreading inland from the coast of California, (2) living near trade routes such as the Old Spanish Trail, frequented by Indian slavers, and (3) being relatively close to the Spanish missions of San Gabriel and San Fernando, sometimes being forced into these missions. These Vanyume and Kitanemuk taken to Mission San Fernando became Fernandiños; others taken to San Gabriel became Gabrieleños and after Americans occupied southern California, they were San Fernando Band of Mission Indians; the Serranos being called San Manuel Band of Mission Indians.

In a 2004 salvage excavation of a burial site (in the way of a 5000-home planned development in southwestern Antelope Valley) monitors from San Fernando Band of Mission Indians were local Indian monitors. In gravesites #2 and #4 (LAN) 949, with elders' approval, scientists extracted DNA from two teeth. The DNA MATCHED ONE OF THE MONITORS—DONNA YOCUM! In March 2006, with permission of the Elders, the bones were blessed and repatriated back to the earth.

Research by Dr. John Johnson of Santa Barbara Natural History Museum also showed that Yocum's ancestors came from a Mojave Desert rancheria, and detailed church records gave the years and names of two of her female ancestors taken from the desert and baptized by San Fernando Mission.

These documented Vanyume are contributing citizens of their current communities.

At the Mojave River Valley Museum Annual BBQ in 2006 in Barstow, the museum honored Chairman John Valenzuela and Yocum with a ceremony and a cake saying "Welcome Home." There were many teary eyes in the audience.

*   *   *

All Those that Wonder Are Not Lost!

by John Valenzuela, Chairman
San Fernando Band of Mission Indians
Seven Feathers Corporation
Hesperia, 2009

It is with great honor and inspiration for me and my fellow tribal members to know that our road to where we came from is finally here. DNA done on one tribal member recently with a DNA from a burial, matched ancient bones found in the Mojave Desert. The road has not been an easy one, but we can now see the light at the end of the tunnel. This has inspired us to know that we are from the Mojave Desert and the San Bernardino Mountains and we are not extinct. Our Vanyume (tribe name) also have Serrano, Tatavian, and Kitanamuk heritage.

I remember being young when my dad would tell us stories and that we were Indian. He thought we were Chumash, because the area where we lived, there were many Chumash living. We learned Chumash songs and stories and traditions.

After my career of working in the labor movement for 40 years, I started my next endeavor. That was to find our correct roots, so that my family could be proud of their heritage. During this time, our family had the opportunity of starting a museum, the Chumash Interpretive Center in Santa Barbara. With the help of Dr. John Johnson, ethnohistorian for the Santa Barbara Natural History Museum, we found that out family was Fernandeño from Mission San Fernando. By this time we had contacted other members of the family, from all over the country, and decided to continue the struggle. In the meantime Donna Yocum (DNA subject) and Marie Mia continued to investigate more facts. Our process is still not complete, but we know where our history started. It has been a hard task having to tell the government we still exist. Remember: All those that wonder are not lost.

Vanyume Leaders--these are leaders of the once considered extinct tribe, the Vanyume. Left to right; Chairman John Valenzuela of the San Fernando Band of Mission Indians; Dr. Phil Walker of Santa Barbara , a forensic archaeologist who did the DNA testing on a Vanyume burial, hundreds of years old, in the Mojave Desert; Donna Yocum, Vice Cochairwoman; and Marie Martinez Mia, Treasurer.

Appendix B

You Did Not Become No More

Repatriation Ceremony March 11, 2006
by Donna Smith Yocum, Vice Cochairwoman
San Fernando Band of Mission Indians

Many Vanyume and Kitanemuk taken from the Mojave Desert and forced into Mission San Fernando were then called Fernandeño and those that were placed at Mission San Gabriel would become known as Gabrieleño.

After secularization when missions were sold, leased, or granted to Californians, Indians were again forced to assimilate into the communities with those which were now living and owning the Indians' homelands. Many scattered, worked at missions or ranchos with yet some escaping back to the mountains or desert.

For generations these people and families survived, laboring at many different levels including ranch hands, vaqueros, and servants. In spite of the horrendous hardships these people faced from the mission era, several families have descendants still living in their ancestral territories, still gathering together just as each prior generation.

It is uncertain as to why many historians wrote off the Vanyume as becoming extinct in the 1900s, but as time has allowed, this misconception is now being corrected. Although they had no choice as to their demise during the mission era, the descendants of the Vanyume continue to live today. One particular group which has evolved into the San Fernando Band of Mission Indians is currently seeking Federal recognition to restore the acknowledgement and sovereignty of their people.

Although not recognized by the government, the San Fernando Band of Mission Indians functions as a tribe with a tribal government consisting of Tribal Council, Tribal Elders Council, Business Council, Cultural Resources Committee and a non profit 501 (c) 3. They have their own governing document (constitution) and bi-laws, which are fully implemented. The tribe consists of nearly 700 documented tribal members. As there were tribal leaders from the mission era, so are there today. With different people in leadership roles over time, it has been through the leadership and guidance of Chairman John Valenzuela,

Vice Chairwoman Donna Smith Yocum and Treasurer Marie Martinez Mia that have led the tribe to where it is in most recent times. Although there are regular tribal elections for the San Fernando Band of Mission Indians, these three people have been consecutively elected over the past thirteen years.

As with many tribes today, the San Fernando Band of Mission Indians has tribal members which have been trained and educated regarding preservation of cultural resources. These tribal members are called Native American Monitors. Their task is to observe and participate in protecting sensitive sites that may be in danger of destruction due to development, construction, potential vandalism, etc. In early 2004 while monitoring a housing development, Native American Monitors from the San Fernando Band of Mission Indians along with archaeologists discovered what would turn out to be a historical discovery. Although this site had been recorded in earlier years, what was to happen next would turn out to be unprecedented. Six burial sites were discovered while excavating for a roadway. After the proper tribal protocol, the remains were secured until repatriation could take place and it was agreed to allow a small extraction of DNA taken from teeth for forensic study by Dr. Phil Walker. Earlier in the 1980s Dr. John Johnson, ethno-historian and curator of anthropology at Santa Barbara Museum of Natural History, took a DNA sample from tribal Elder Lydia Cooke Manriquez (now deceased) and years later from Donna Smith Yocum (grand-niece of Lydia Manriquez), and recorded it with other DNA results for research he was conducting. The two-mitochondrial DNA results were identical.

DNA extracted from the remains discovered at excavation site were an identical match as Vice-Chairwoman Donna Yocum and her deceased Aunt Lydia Manriquez, who are direct descendents of the Vanyume as are many in the tribe, and all the remaining are directly related. San Fernando Band of Mission Indians can show through mission records and other documentation that their ancestors came from the Mojave Desert and Antelope Valley with documentation showing names, tribal villages and dates of baptisms, marriages and deaths of each of their (Vanyume) ancestors dating back to the 1700s, with a genealogy unbroken down to the today's generations and mitochondrial DNA that cannot be disputed. The San Fernando Band of Mission Indians continues to exist; therefore the Vanyume live.

These surviving families are a part of a tragic American epic—only now with some joy: the Vanyume are not extinct.

Prayer

Repatriation Ceremony
March 11, 2006
By Marie Martinez Mia, Treasurer

Creator God,
Thank you for allowing us all to be here today. You know the importance and role of each person here today and how each has been involved in bringing these ancestors back to us. Creator, we know that you had revealed your plan to these special ancestors. They knew of their disturbed rest. They were waiting to meet us, their grandchildren, and to prove to the world the importance of our lineage. They knew this reconnection would be validated for all to know. Ancestors, we apologize for this disturbance, yet with our deepest love we thank you for this sacrifice. Please accept these humble offerings from your children, and may you now truly rest in peace. Creator, please bestow your many blessings on all of us gathered here today and continue to watch over us, your children, on this special road you have put before us.

Amen. *Aho* to all my relations.

Words to My Ancestors

Given at
Repatriation Ceremony
March 11, 2006
By Donna Smith Yocum

You have been with us all along …. You had been watching us in spirit and you heard our tears.

You heard us crying ...how can we make them know who we really are?

How can we show them who we are?

How can we show them you did not become no more, for you walk within us...we are the same people?

You brought us to this place ...You came to us ... You could have called out to any number of others...

But you called us.

And then...You gave us the most enormous gift, a proof undeniable....

You gave us the undisputable identity we needed. Not many can claim such an honorable identity.

It was your desire even through your disrupted peace, for everyone to know who you were
and that we are yours....
We are the same, you walk within us.

You ask us to protect you and those before us...you tell us to protect ourselves and who we are...

You tell us to never let these things be taken from us...
and in your honor....

We will do these things you ask of us...always...and forever.

I say to my beloved ancestors...thank you. Please accept our humble prayers, our gifts and our love.

Go now and once again sing and dance....

As we will sing in our hearts with you.... and in spirit...dance with you.

Peace forevermore my family...until we meet again.

Scars left on the desert floor, remnant of the Old Spanish Trail (mule trail) from 1830-1848, north of I-15 looking southwest toward the Mojave River, where caravans of New Mexican traders brought blankets to trade for California horses and mule, but along these trails came horse thieves and Indian slave traders, causing untold human scars

Appendix C

Chronology of Slave Laws

1500s—Spain: "possession of all acquired territory was vested in the Crown of Spain" rather than the government.

King treated citizens like padres treated Indians. Like feudal system: Pope granted land to the King of Spain and king granted like vassalage to certain people.

Hispaniola: the Spanish had rights to enforce natives to yield or be consigned to slavery. Spain had right to hold and possess.

Defeated Indians in Hispaniola offered to serve Spain if they could live their old ways—[pathetic plea of surrender—author].

1511—King Ferdinand vested power and control under the King of Spain in Council of the Indies. This was perfected by Charles I in 1524. Charles V of Spain enacted *Leyes Nueves,* New Laws, i.e., Indians are humans and should be protected by the Crown.

1538—Pope Paul III forbade all enslavement.

!542—Spanish law allowed natives to be parceled out to "teach things of our holy Catholic faith."

1542-1563--The king granted land, a *repartimiento,* "to have, to hold, and to possess." At first nothing was said about Indians on that land but soon natives were parceled like cattle, to till the soil, quite like European feudal systems: "To you, such a one, is given an *encomienda* of so many Indians with such a *cacique,* and you are to teach them the things of our holy Catholic faith."

Spain used *encomienda* which gave Spaniards right to the land and control over Indians on that land. Control meant Spaniards could require a share of products produced or labor "volunteered" each month or year. Owners sometimes let Indians work for someone else, such as a silver miner. About this time 160,000 Indians worked in silver mines.

1548—No slavery allowed in New Spain—hardly enforced!

1550s—Bartolomé de las Casas worked with Charles V to help the cause of Indians in the New World.

At Cigales king granted that Indians in New Mexico could have land around the Pueblos so that their herds could be kept separate from the Spanish animals.

1551 Spanish authorities nominally freed slaves but mine workers continued to work; officials sentenced prisoners to labor in the mines.

1563—Recapitulation of *Leyes de los Reinos de las Indies.*

1589—Spanish laws stated Indians should not be forced to work; volunteering was okay.

1597—Juan de Oñate granted *encomiendas* to New Mexican colonists .

1619—One of America's important years in history: Slaves were bought at Jamestown, Virginia, from Dutch ship; House of Burgesses meets for 1ˢᵗ American colonial legislature; and for good and bad [?] women were sold to men in Jamestown for about 100 pounds of tobacco each, giving America its first nicotine fit.

1709—French Royal Edict of 1709 sanctioned slavery in Canada among Native Americans.

1745--French Royal Council sanctioned Indian slavery

1700s—Indian women used more by the Spanish colonist than English or French colonists.

1800s (early)—Some Africa slaves wanted to die in African ports or on slave voyages, because their souls might be released to go back to their homeland in Africa.

1767—Expulsion of Jesuits. Greatest blow to Indians.

1778—*Provincias Internas* became the government for the northern provinces of New Spain. Juan Bautista de Anza became governor of New Mexico under this new organization.

1778-- A *Bando* prohibiting trading with Ute Indians in northern New Mexico and Utah. Not enforced well.

1700-1800s—typical attitude of Europeans and American whites that slavery is doing blacks and Indians a service because slavery helped civilize primitive people; therefore European slaves would not have to live in primitive conditions—sometimes saving their souls too.

1808--Importation of African slaves in the United States is prohibited—making Negro slaves more valuable.

1824--Mexican California prohibits trade in Indian captives.

1820s--Trappers come to Taos and find that Spanish have a market for Indian slaves and horses (demand for horses might be challenged as assumptions are that horses are plentiful in New Spain—author confused on this point)

1820--Missouri Compromise: After Missouri became a slave state, no slavery allowed in the western territory above 36° 30'

1829--Republic of Mexico prohibits slavery.

1830s--California missions easy prey for obtaining slave women to sell.

1834--Slavery abolished in British Empire.

1848--Treaty of Guadalupe Hildalgo in 1848, included regulation for stopping slavers going into Mexico to take Mexicans and Indians as slaves and bringing them back to the United States.

1849—California 1st State Constitution, Art. I, Sec. 18, Slavery was prohibited.

1850s-1865--California Indentured laws 1850 to the 1860s California kept revising laws concerning Indians, basically restricting them, justifying murdering and kidnapping for slaves, expelling them from their centuries-old homes. Rules and lack of laws and lack of human enforcement of laws made to protect Indians led to near extinction and genocide. In 1863 Negroes could exercise their rights by testifying in court, whereas Indians still could not (see chapter 8).

1853--Gov. Brigham Young proclaimed that New Mexicans could not trade in slaves in the Utah Territory. This was followed by the territorial legislature passing the same. Utah law allowed Mormons to buy captives "out of slavery." Indians then became indentured to a Mormon family and brought up as a Mormon and treated for the most part as a member of the family.

1854--Missouri Compromise invalidated with the Kansas-Nebraska Act, allowing territories to choose whether they want Negro slavery or not.

1863, Jan. 1--President A. Lincoln abolished slavery in the still rebellious Southern States, not Negro slaves in Kentucky, Maryland or Delaware.

1865--Amendment XIII--Dec. 1865-- "Neither slavery or involuntary servitude…" Prohibits slavery in the United States. President Andrew Johnson ordered the end of Indian slave trade.

1867—Peonage system is abolished in New Mexico, but many slaves and indentured Indians remain with families.

1860s—New Mexican trials to free Indian slaves from bondage had mixed results, freeing some, denying others, with some freed people deciding to remain with New Mexican families or with enslaving Indians. A Ute slave, for example, living with the Navajos for years decided to remain with her Navajo family.

1900s—Slavery vestiges remained in New Mexico.

1900s (late)—people looked up their roots to find blood lines and find some traces of slavery background. Indians intermarried frequently so mixed tribal marriages were common. Increasing pride of being part Indian spread through the United States.

Chapter Notes

Preface

1. William R. Palmer, *Pahute Indian Legends* (Salt Lake City: Deseret Books Company Publishers, 1946), ix. "Gone the Way of the Earth" comes from Palmer's Preface about the old Paiute informants who have passed away, "gone the way of the earth." For years now all the people involved in Indian slavery in the Southwest, victims and perpetrators, are all gone the way of the earth.

Chapter 1

The Southwest and Indian Slavery

1. Frank W. Blackmar, *Spanish Institutions of the Southwest* (Glorieta: The Rio Grande Press, Inc., 1976), 56-62.
2. George Brown Tindall and David Emory Shi, *American: A Narrative History* (New York: W. W. Norton & Company, 2007), 31-32; Charles Gibson, *Spain in America* (New York: Harper Torchbooks, 1966), 52-68. Gibson explains the *encomienda* system and the history of it, especially how it changed from use in the West Indies to Mexico (New Spain); Frank Waters, *Masked Gods: Navaho and Pueblo Ceremonialism* (New York: Ballentine Books, 1873), 29, 70.
3. James F. Brooks, "Captive, Concubine, Servant, Kin: A Historian Divines Experience in Archaeological Slaveries," in Catherine M. Cameron, editor, *Invisible Citizens: Captives and their Consequences* (Salt Lake City: The University of Utah Press, 2008), 285; Debra L. Martin, "Ripped Flesh and Torn Souls: Skeletal Evidence for Captivity and Slavery from the La Plata Valley, New Mexico, AD 1100-1300," in Catherine M. Cameron, editor, *Invisible Citizens: Captives and their Consequences* (Salt lake City: The University of Utah Press, 2008), 159-80.

4. Catherine M. Cameron, "Captives in Prehistory as Agents of Social Change," in Catherine M. Cameron, editor, *Invisible Citizens: Captives and their Consequences* (Salt Lake City: The University of Utah Press, 2008), 11-20.

5. Sally Crum, *People of the Red Earth: American Indians of Colorado* (Santa Fe: Ancient City Press, 1996), 139, 143, 167-68, 174-75.

6. *Ibid.*

7. Allen Lonnberg, "The Digger Indian Stereotype in California," *Journal of California and Great Basin Anthropology*, Vol. 3, No. 2, 1981, 215-16; Carobeth Laird, *The Chemehuevis* (Banning: Malki Press, 1976); Forrest S. Cuch, *A History of Utah's American Indians* (Salt Lake City: Utah State Department of Indian Affairs, 2003). Cuch's authentic book has a wealth of information on the Paiutes and Utes throughout the state, their legends, background and relationships with each other before and after some obtained the horse culture. It is more honest in relations between Mormon and Indians and the negative treatment of Indians by the Mormons.

8. Paiute, also Pah-ute, Piute, Pah-Utahs, Pied, Piede and more. Clifford E. Trafzer and Joel R. Hyer, editors. *Exterminate Them—Written Accounts of the Murder, Rape, and Enslavement of Native Americans During the California Gold Rush, 1848-1868* (East Lansing: Michigan State University Press, 1999), 159-180. "Exterminate Them" contains dozens of newspaper articles and letters from 1850 to 1868 showing the brutality of the treatment of and attitude toward California Indians.

9. Lonnberg, "The Digger Indian Stereotype in California," 216; *George C. Yount & his Chronicles of the West,* edited by Charles L. Camp (Denver: Old West Publishing Company, 1966), 73. This is a fascinating book, describing Indians of the west and tales of adventures and trapping. It is an enlightening book to learn about the Old West. See also Trafzer's *Exterminate Them* for use of "Digger" in California documents.

10. Dale L. Morgan, *Jedehiah Smith and the Opening of the West* (Lincoln: University of Nebraska Press, 1964), 337, 197, 210, 227.

11. Warren A. Beck, *New Mexico: A History of Four Centuries* (Norman: University of Oklahoma Press, 1926), 84.

12. William Brandon, *The American Handbook of Indians* (New York: Dell Publishing Co., 1964), 128; Thomas E. Sheridan and Nancy J. Parezo, editors, *Paths of Life: American Indians of the Southwest and Northern Mexico* (Tucson: The University of Arizona Press, 1996), 148.

13. Frank Waters, *The Book of the Hopi* (New York: The Viking Press, 1963) 258-69; James F. Brooks, "Captive, Concubine, Servant, Kin: A Historian Divines Experience in Archaeological Slaveries," in Catherine M. Cameron, editor, *Invisible Citizens: Captives and their Consequences*, 287; Harold Courlander, *The Fourth World of the Hopis: The Epic Story of the Hopi Indians as Preserved in their Legends and Traditions* (Albuquerque: University of New Mexico Press, 1971), 275-84.

14. *Ibid.*

15. Waters, *The Book of the Hopi*, 268-69; Brandon, *The American Handbook*, 123.

16. _____ Galbaith, "Turbulent Taos" (Denver: The Press of the Territories), Number 18, 1970. This is Number 18 of a *Series of Western Americana*, 5-6, 10-12.

Chapter 2

The Mojave Indians and Slavery

1. The accepted spelling of the Indian tribe is *Mohave* or *Mojave,* singular and plural, whereas the river and desert have assumed the Spanish spelling of *Mojave.* In Arizona the common spelling is Mohave. John C. Fremont named the river *Mohahve,* placing that on his 1844 survey map.

2. On August 6, 1806, the Indians around Bakersfield told Lieutenant Francisco Maria Ruiz and Father Jose Maria Zalvidea of Santa Barbara Mission and presidio that the *Majagua* (Mohave) Indians came to this spot to trade. Details were even added as to the scarcity of water during the ten-day journey. Other Spanish documents show them as far north as Missions

San Miguel and San Luis Obispo.

3. Jesse D. Stockton, *Spanish Trailblazers in the South San Joaquin 1772-1816* (Bakersfield: Kern County Historical Society, 1957), 1. George William Beattie and Helen Pruitt Beattie, *Heritage of the Valley, San Bernardino's First Century* (Pasadena: San Pasqual Press, 1939), 2.

4. Elliot Coues, *On the Trail of a Spanish Pioneer, the Diary and itinerary of Francisco Garces (Missionary Priest) in his travels through Sonora, Arizona, and California, 1775-1776,Translated from an Official Contemporaneous Copy of the Original Spanish Manuscript, and Edited with Copious Notes in Two Volumes* (New York: Francis P. Harper, 1900), I, 216-17, 248.

5. The Halchidhoma was one of the weaker Colorado River tribes of Yuman linguistic stock living near the present town of Parker. Garces referred to them as *Jalcheduns*. Mojave and Quechan expelled them from the Colorado in the 1850s by the joint effort and the Halchidhoma moved to the Gila River near the Mariposa Indians. Chemehuevis Indians moved to part of the Halchidhoma territory on the Colorado River.

6. R.B. Stratton, *Captivity of the Oatman Girls* (Salem: Oregon Teachers Monthly, 1909), Chapter XVI. Although this source has been proven to be weak in historical facts and overly romantic, it does give insight to Mojave life and customs. Grant Foreman, ed., *A Pathfinder in the Southwest: The Itinerary of Lieutenant A. W. Whipple during his explorations for a railway route from Fort Smith to Los Angeles in the years 1853 and 1854* (Norman: University of Oklahoma Press, 1941), 237. See also Whipple, 127, for another example of Mexican slavery in Central New Mexico. See also Carolyn Niethammer, *Daughters of the Earth: The Lives and Legends of American Indian Women* (Simon and Schuster, Inc. 1955), 182-83.

7. Stratton, *Captivity*, 226; A. L. Kroeber, "Olive Oatman Return," *Anthropological Society Papers*, No. 4 (Berkeley1950), 1-8; for another verizon for this captive Cocopah woman named Nowereha, see page 183 of Niethammer, *Daughters of the Earth*.

8. Stratton, *Captivity*, 213-217.

9. Kroeber, "Oatman Return,"1-8.

10. A. L. Kroeber, and Clifton B. Kroeber, "Olive Oatman's First Account of Her Captivity Among the Mohave," *California Historical Society Quarterly* (no date, copy in possession of author), 309-17; this monogram is an analysis of Olive Oatman's interview by Captain Martin Burke of Ft. Yuma in February, 1856, when the Mojave returned her to the Americans; Brandon, *The American Handbook, 128*; Cecilia Rasmussen, "Tale of Kindness Didn't Fit Notion of Savage Indian," *Los Angeles Times*, July 16, 2000; Richard Dillon, "Tragedy at Oatman Flat: Massacre, Captivity, Mystery," *The American West,* March/April, 1981; Lynn Galvin, "Cloudwoman: The Life of Olive Oatman, An Old California Indian Captive," *The Californians,* Volume 13, n. 2, nd.

11 Kroeber and Kroeber, "Olive Oatman's First Account."

12. Dillon, "Tragedy at Oatman Flat."

13. Foreman, ed., *A Pathfinder in the Southwest: The Itinerary of Lieutenant A. W. Whipple during his explorations for a railway route from Fort Smith to Los Angeles in the years 1853 and 1854.*

14. Thomas E. Sheridan and Nancy J. Parezo, *Paths of Life: American Indians*, 221-25.

Chapter 3

California Slavery under Spain and Mexico

1. Fray Zephyrin Engelhardt, *San Gabriel Mission and the Beginnings of Los Angeles* (San Gabriel, 1927), 19.

2. Martha Menchaca, *Recovering History Constructing Race: The Indians, Black and White--Roots of Mexican Americans* (Austin: University of Texas, 2001), 141.

3. Susanna Bryant Daking, *A Scotch Paisano - Hugo Reid's Life in California, 1832-1852, Derived from His Correspondence* (Berkeley: University of California Press, 1939), 265.

4. Engelhardt, *San Gabriel Mission,* 13.

5. Maurice S. Sullivan, *The Travels of Jedediah Smith* (Santa Ana: The Fine Arts Press, 1934), 169, n 68.

6. Don José Del Carmen Lugo, "Vida de un Rancho," dictated to Thomas Savage, 1877, translated by Helen Pruitt Beattie, *Quarterly of San Bernardino County Museum Association* (Winter, 1961), 36; *Minute Book of the Illustrious Ayuntamiento, II,* session of February 11, 1837,MSS, Official Translation in the Los Angeles City Clerk's Office; H.H. Bancroft, *The History of California* (San Francisco: The History Company, 1884), III, 622 n. 16, 643 n. 9; Thomas J. Farnham, *Adventures in California,* Pictorial Edition (New York: No publisher listed in rebound copy at University of Southern California Library, 1849),346. Farnham estimated that California ranges held one million black cattle, 500,000 horses and 3,000 mules.

7. Burrill, *River of Sorrows,* 158-60. Burrill gives details of Sutter's relationships with Indians, both good and bad.

8. A.L.Kroeber, "Yurok Law and Custom," in *The California Indians, A Source Book,* edited by R.F. Heizer and M.A. Whipple (Berkeley: University of California Press, 1971), 28, 395-96, 399, 404-05; Philip Drucker. *Indians of the North Coast* (Garden City: The Natural History Press, 1963), 18, 31; Carolyn Niethammer, *Daughters of the Earth: The Lives and Legends of American Indian Women.* (Simon and Schuster, Inc. 1955), 180. http://www.simonsays.com/content/book.cfm?tab=1&pid=407274.

9. Thomas N. Layton, "Traders and Raiders: Aspects of Trans-Basin and California—Plateau Commerce 1800-1830," *Journal of California and Great Basin Anthropology,* Vol. 3, no. 1, 1981, 127-132; Jack D. Forbes, *Native Americans of California and Nevada: A Handbook* (Healdsburg: Naturegraph Publishers, 1969), 42, 73-74; Colin F. Taylor and William C. Sturtevant. *The Native Americans: The Indigenous People of North America* (New York: Smithmark Publishing Inc., 1996),197-98.

10. Ibid.

11. Layton, "Traders and Raiders,"129-134.

12. Ruth Underhill, The*Northern Paiute Indians of California and Nevada* (Branch of Indian Affairs, Bureau of Indian Affairs, 1941), 55.

13. Layton, "Traders and Raiders,"128-134

14. Maurice S. Sullivan, *The Travels of Jedediah Smith,* 107, 120, 125, 135.

15. Layton, "Traders and Raiders," 128-135.

16. Fray Zephyrin Engelhardt, *The Missions and Missionaries of California* (San Francisco: James H. Barry Company, 1913), III, 31. A slightly different version of the fight was described in Charles E. Chapman, *A History of California: The Spanish Period* (New York: the Macmillan Company, 1936), 433.

17. Engelhardt, *The Missions and Missionaries of California*, III, 35.

18. *Ibid.*, III, 38; Beattie and Beattie. *Heritage of the Valley*, 1939), 6-7; Fr. Joaquin Pasquel Nuez. *Diary of Fr. Joaquin Pasquel Nuez, Minister of San Gabriel and Chaplain of the Expedition Against the Mojave Indian, Begun by Lieutenant Gabriel Moraga, Novenber 1819*. Translated by George Beattie. Copy in Walker's *Back Door to California: The Story of the Mojave River Trail*, Appendix C. Also in Huntington Library

19. Engelhardt, *Missions and Missionaries of California*, III, 35-39.

20. John C. Fremont, *Memories of My Life* (New York: Belford, Clarke and Company, 1887) I, 362; Brevet Col. J. C. Fremont, *The Exploring Expeditions to the Rocky Mountains, Oregon and California* (Buffalo: Geo. Derby & Co.Publishers, 1849), 376-77; Brevet Col. J. C. Fremont, *The Exploring Expeditions to the Rocky Mountains in the Year 1842 and to Oregon and Northern California in Year 1843-44.* in *Public Documents*, by Order of the Senate of the U.S., 2nd Session of the 28 Congress XI (Washington: 1845), 260-62; Clifford J. Walker, *Back Door to California: The Story of the Mojave River Trail* (Barstow: Mojave River Valley Museum, 1986), 53.

21.David Earle, Personal interview, Barstow, January 2007.

Chapter 4

Continuing Slavery in New Mexico

1. Elizabeth von Till Warren, "Brutal Barter: Indian Slave Trade in the Great Basin 1710-1880," *Spanish Traces* Vol. 7, No.1, Spring 2001 (Old Spanish Trail Association).

2. Patricia, Kuhlhoff, Telephone interview, New Mexico, Sep-

tember 28, 2008.

3. Warren, "Brutal Barter," 9-10; Sondra Jones, *The Trial of Don Pedro León Luján: The Attack Against Indian Slavery and Mexican Trade in Utah* (Salt Lake City: University of Utah Press, 1949), 38-39, 53; *"Genízaro" in New Mexico Historic Review,* volume unknown, 70, includes the definitions and history of the word, in possession of the author.

4. Joseph P. Sanchez, *Explorers, Traders, and Slavers: Forging the Old Spanish Trail* (Salt Lake City: University of Utah Press, 1997), 91-2; Leroy R. Hafen and Ann W. Hafen, eds., *The Old Spanish Trail: Santa Fe to Los Angeles with Extracts from Contemporary Records and Including Diaries of Antonio Armijo and Orville Pratt, of the Far West and the Rockies Historical Series 1820-1875* (Glendale: The Arthur H. Clark Company, 1954), I, 280.

5. Warren, "Brutal Barter," 10; Frank McNitt *The Indian Trader* (Norman: University of Oklahoma Press, 1962), 17.

7. Sanchez, *Explorers, traders, and Slavers*, 95.

8. Estevan Real-Galvez, *Identifying Captivity and Capturing Indentity: Narratives of American   Indians Slavery in New Mexico and Colorado, 1776-1934,* a dissertation University of Michigan 2002, 164.

9. Rael-Galvez, *Identifying Captivity,* 59, 88-89.

10. Rael-Galvez, *Identifying Captivity,* 88.

11. Paul Bailey, *Walkara, Hawk of the Mountains* (Los Angeles: Westernlore Press, 1954), 149; Leland Hargrave Creer, "Spanish—American Slave Trade in the Great Basin, 1800-1853," *New Mexico Historical Review,* Vol. XXXIV, July 1949, No. 3, 178-9; McNitt, *The Indian Slave Trader,* 17-18.

Chapter 5

A Strange Marriage—Utes and Mormons

1. Creer, "Spanish—American Slave Trade in the Great Basin,"

179-80.

2. Edward Leo Lyman, *The Overland Journey from Utah to California: Wagon Travel from the City of the Saints to the City of the Angels* (Reno: University of Nevada Press, 2004). This classic of the trail from Salt Lake to Los Angeles has the best exposition of the Mormon and Indian relationships along the trail south of Salt Lake. The Mormons maintained peaceful intercourse with the Indians to avoid losses while traveling.

3. Gottfredson, *History Indian Depredations in Utah,*16-19.

4. Creer, "Spanish—American Slave Trade in the Great Basin," 181.

5. Gottfredson, *History Indian Depredations in Utah,* 15-17.

6. Hafen and Hafen, *The Old Spanish Trail,* 278, n. 25, 279. See Cuch, *A History of Utah's American Indians* for more details of both good and bad treatment of Indians under the Mormons.

7. *Ibid.,* 280.

8. *Ibid.,* 280-83.

Chapter 6

Glimpses of Mexican Slavery in California

1. Robert Heizer, "Impact of Colonization on the Native Californian Societies," *The Journal of San Diego History*, Winter 1978, Volume 24, No. 1, 14-15, http:www.sandiegohistory.org/journal/78/impact.htm ; Walker, *Back Door to California*, 71.

2. Beattie, *Heritage of the Valley*, 11. ???

3. Menchaca, *Recovering History Constructing Race* p161; Goodrich, Chauncey Shafter. *The Legal Status of the California Indian*, Reprint from *California Law Review*, January-March, 1926 (San Francisco), 6.

4. Harrison C. Dale, ed., *The Ashley-Smith Exploration and*

Discovery of the Central Route to the Pacific, 1822-1829 (Cleveland: the Arthur H. Clark Company, 1918), 189, 190, 198-200.

5. *Ibid.,* 213, 217,219, 204-05.

6. Robert Heizer, "Impact of Colonization on the Native Californian Societies," 14-5; Sherburne Cook, "Franciscan Missionaries," nd, publisher unknown, 26-27, copy in possession of author. This list gives reasons by 30 Indians for running away from the mission in San Francisco in 1797; Clifford J. Walker, *Back Door to California: The Story of the Mojave River Trail* (Barstow: Mojave River Valley Museum Association, 1986), 124-125.

7. Robert Heizer, "Impact of Colonization on the Native Californian Societies."

8. Dale, *Ashley-Smith Explorations,* 199ff.

9. Hill, Joseph J. "Ewing Young in the Fur Trade of the Far Southwest, 1822-1834," reprint from *Oregon Historical Quarterly,* XXIV, No. 1 (Eugene: Koke-Tiffnay Co., 1923), 9, 11, 14, 21,[[[? Fram p. 96 ?] .

10. Walker, *Back Door to California,* 124-125.

11. McNitt, *The Indian Slave Trader,* 23; John L. Jorgensen, "Spanish Traders and American Trappers," from *A History of Castle Valley to 1890,* a masters thesis, 1955, 15-16, from Emery County Archives. Castle Dale, Utah.

12. LeRoy R. Hafen and Ann W. Hafen, eds., *The Old Spanish Trail: Santa Fe to Los Angeles with Extracts from Contemporary Records and Including Diaries of Antonio Armijo and Orville Pratt, of the Far West and the Rockies Historical Series 1820-1875* (Glendale: The Arthur H. Clark Company, 1954), I, 53; Warren A. Beck, *New Mexico: A History of Four Centuries* (Norman: University of Oklahoma Press, 1926),183; Walker, *Back Door to California,* 96-106.

13. Bailey, *Walkara, Hawk of the Mountains,* 147, 149.

14. *Ibid.*

15. Sanchez, *Explorers, traders, and Slavers,* 125-27.

16. John Brown Jr. and James Boyd, *History of San Bernardino and Riverside Counties* (Chicago: Western Historical Association, 1922), I, 28-29.

17. Encomiendero

18. Dakin, *Hugo Reid's Life in California,* 124. For Wilson's complete memoirs see Robert Glass Cleland, *Pathfinders* (Los Angeles: Powell Publishing Company, 1929).

19. Juan Bautista Esparza, *Vida California, 1834-47,* MS California Archives C D, p. 44. Microfilm at Los Angeles County Museum, original in Bancroft Library, Berkeley.

20. John Charles Fremont, *Memoirs of My Life* (Chicago: Belford, Clarke & Company, 1887), I, 370-376; Walker, *Back Door to California,* 134-135. Fremont's 1844 trip out of California on the Old Spanish Trail came across an ambushed group of New Mexican traders at Resting Springs. Horses were taken, men were killed and women captured. Kit Carson and Alex Goday rescued about half the horses in a 100-mile trip in 30 hours. Fremont called it "the boldest and most disinterested" exploit in the west. Well, Carson and Goday found Indians with the horses 60 miles from Resting Springs taken by different Paiutes who came across the horses at Bitter Springs. They were, indeed, cooking one horse but did ambush the New Mexicans at Resting Springs. They only found all these four-footed protein meat where two New Mexican left them at Bitter Springs. Carson and Goday killed two Indian men and rescued about a dozen horses, but punished the wrong Indians. Read *Back Door to California* for a more detail account.

21. Bailey, *Walkara, Hawk of the Mountains,* 46-47.

Chapter 7

Eye Witnesses on the Trail and California

1. Hafen, *Old Spanish Trail,* I, 52, n. 9.The Pratt Diary is through courtesy of the Cole Collection of Western Americana, Yale University Library.

2. William B. Lorton, *The Diaries of William B. Lorton: September 1848 - January 1850,* MSS, C-F 190 Bancroft Library, Berkeley, California, 184. "Piede" it is a mixture of Indian and Spanish, according to Lorton's definition, Walkara was called by many names: Wak, Walker, Wakara, Waker.

3. *Ibid.,*184, 193. Lorton repeatedly referred to "Wms" and Williams Rancho Chino in Southern California. Isaac Williams received part of his rancho in December, 1841, from Antonio Maria Lugo, his father-in-law.

4. *Minute Book of the Illustrious Ayuntamiento Census of 1836 and 1844,* III, MSS, Official Translation in the Los Angeles City Clerk's Office; Walker, *Back Door to California,* 117.

5. Paul Bailey, *Walkara, Hawk of the Mountains,*(Los Angeles: Westernlore Press, 1954), 31.

6. Lorton, *The Diaries of William B. Lorton,*208.

7. D. Bonner, ed., *The Life and Adventures of James P. Beckwourth* (New York: Alfred A. Knoph, 1931), 348-49.

8. J. Farnham, *Adventures in California with Travels in Oregon,* Pictorial Edition (New York: No publisher listed in rebound copy at University of Southern California Library, 1849), 377.

9. Beck, *History of New Mexico,* 183.

10. Farnham, *Adventures in California with Travels in Oregon,* p. 378.

11. LeRoy Hafen and Ann W. Hafen, ed., *Central Route to the Pacific by Gwinn Harris Heap with Related Material on Railroad Explorations and Indian Affairs, by Edward F. Beale, Thomas H. Benton, Kit Carson, and Col. I. A. Hitchcock, and in Other Documents, 1853-54* (Glendale: The Arthur H. Clark Company, 1957), 235. This volume contains a reprint of Heap's journal which was first printed in 1854; Charles Wood. Chemehuevi Chairman, MMS., "Convocation of 14th Annual Old Spanish Trail Conference," Barstow, June 8, 2007, in possession of author.

12. *Minute Book of the Illustrious Ayuntamiento Census of 1836 and 1844,* III, MSS.

13. *Los Angeles Plaza Church Death Records,* translated through the courtesy of William Mason, Los Angeles County Museum.

14. Michael Claringbud White, *California All The Way Back To 1828* (Los Angeles: G. Dawson: 1956), 44. Michael White stated he returned to California with the Workman-Rowland party and reached the Cajon Pass on Christmas Day; Walker, *Back Door to California*, 118-19.

15. *Ibid.*

16. Muscubiabe (No. 75) Transcript of proceeding before U.S. Land Commission. Michael White. Document 79, Beattie Collection, Huntington Library.

Chapter 8

Americans Take Over

1. S. Garfielde and F. A. Snyder, eds., *Compiled Laws of the State of California, Containing All the Acts of the Legislature of a Public and General Nature, Now in Force, Passed at the Sessions of 1850-51-52-53, To Which Are Prefixed the Declaration of Independence, The Constitution of the United States and of California, the Treaty of Queretaro, and the Nationalization Laws of the United States* (Boston: Franklin Printing House, 1853), 822-824. See also John Walton Caughey, *The Indians of Southern California in 1852; The B.D. Wilson Report and a*

Selection of Contemporary Comment (Los Angeles: The Plantin Press, 1952), 77; Trafzer, "Exterminate Them," 157-58.

2. Charles Francis Saunders and J. Smeaton Chase, *The California Padres and Their Missions* (Boston: Houghton Mifflin Company, 1915), 101; Major Horace Bell, *Reminiscences of a Ranger or Early Times in Southern California* (Santa Barbara: Wallace Hebberd, 1927), 35-36.

3. *Daily Morning Call* (San Francisco), November 24, 1858; Charles Wood, MMS., Chemehuevi Chairman, "Convocation of 14th Annual Old Spanish Trail Conference."

4. Rich Adams, Personal Interview, Roseville, CA, September 19, 2008, Maidu Indian, at Maidu Interpretive Center, Roseville; Secrest, *When the Great Spirit Died*. In 1863 a small pox epidemic killed thousands of California Indians; Richard Burrill, *River of Sorrow: Life History of the Maidu-Nisenan Indians* (Happy Camp, Naturegraph Publishing, Inc., 1988),143-49,215-19. From a population of 8,000-10,000, the Maidu went to 1,100 in 1910, including mixed blood. L. Frank and Kim Hogeland, *First Families: A Photographic History of California Indians* (Berkeley: Heyday Books, 2007), 7.

5. Jack Forbes, *Native Americans of California and Nevada* (Happy Camp, CA: Naturegraph, 2006), 44; Brandon, *C of Indians* 281.

6. Chauncey Shafter Goodrich, *The Legal Status of the California Indian*, Reprint from *California Law Review*, January-March, 1926 (San Francisco), 10-12; Trafzer, *Exterminate Them*, 156-58.

7. *Ibid.*

8. William B. Secrest, *When the Great Spirit Died: The Destruction of the California Indians 1850-1860* (Sanger, CA: World Dancer Press, 2003). Secrest's book has hundreds of documented records of California's ruthless treatment and ex-

ploitation of the Indians.

9. William H. Brewer, *Up and Down California 1860-1864,* editor Francis P. Farquhar (Berkeley: University of California Press, 1966),492-93;

10. F. A. Van Winkle, "The Foremothers Tell of Olden Times," *Gold Rush Stories of Women Pioneers,http://www.sfmuseum. net/hist5/foremoms.html* ?? 3]

11. Lonnberg, "The Digger Indian Stereotype in California," 216.

12. Brewer, *Up and Down California 1860-1864,* 387; Secrest, *When the Great Spirit Died.*

13. Bonnie Ketterl Kane, "A View from Ridge Route," Vol. 1 of *The First People* (Frazier Park, CA: Bonnie's Books. 2001). Researcher Kane did a superb job bringing together primary resources about this triangular mountain area between the Mojave Desert and the San Joaquin Valley and the Santa Barbara Coast, an excellent book about several Indian groups and the pathetic and chaotic attempts to help them in the middle of the 19th century.

14. *Ibid.*

15. Clifford J, Walker, *Los Coyote and the Mojave Desert, MSS, 2006; Goodrich, The Legal Status of the California Indian,"* 13-14; Charles Wood, MSS, "Convocation of 14th Annual Old Spanish Trail Conference," Barstow, June 8, 2007, copy in possession of author.

16. *Ibid.*

17. Warren, "Brutal Barter," 12.

18. Wilcomb E. Washburn, *The American Indian and the United States: A Documentary History,* Vol. I, Smithsonian Institute

(New York: Random House, 1973). This set of volumes has letters and "Reports of Commissioner of Indian Affairs" during the 19th and 20th centuries, 43, 57-58, 76, 102-06, 109, 134, 167.

19. *Ibid.*

20. Mary McD. Gordon, ed. *Through Indian Country to California: John P. Sherburne's Diary of the Whipple Expedition 1853-54* (Stanford: Stanford University Press, 1988), 210, n. 24.

21. Trafzer, *Exterminate Them!,*68-70, 112, 114-15, 1222-24, 126.

22. *Ibid.*

23. *Daily Morning Call* (San Francisco), December 10, 1858.

24. Warren, "Brutal Barter," 14.

25. William Wood Averell, *Ten Years in the Saddle*, Edited by Edward K. Eckert and Nicholas J. Amato (San Rafael: Presidio Press, 1978), 103.

Chapter 9

Finally Slavery Ends

1. McNitt, *The Indian Trader,* 19

2. Bailey, *Walkara, Hawk of the Mountains,* 209-211.

3. Creer, "Spanish—American Slave Trade in the Great Basin, 1800-1853," 182-3.

4. Creer, "Spanish—American Slave Trade in the Great Basin, 1800-1853," 162; Rael-Galvez, *Identifying Captivity and Capturing Indentity*, 183-187; Warren, *"Butal Barter,"* 11; Lafayette Head, "Statement of Mr. Head of Abiqui[u] in regard to buying and selling of Paiute Indian Children April 30, 1852." RI 2150.

Huntington Library, San Marino, CA.

5. "An Act for the Relief of Indian Slaves and Prisoners," passed by the Legislature of the Territory of Utah, January 31, A.D. 1852, located in Appendix of Bailey, *Walkara, Hawk of the Mountains*; Warren, "Brutal Barter," 11.

6. Judicial Cases 329 and 302 respectively, New Mexico State Archives, Sante Fe, New Mexico.

7. Josiah Gregg, *The Commerce of the Prairies by Josiah Gregg*, edited by Milo Milton Quaife (Lincoln: University of Nebraska Press, 1967), 207-11. Gregg commented about his trading with the Comanches, that each Comanche owner of a mule, horse or slave wanted several items in trade, for example, a blanket, looking glass, flint, awl, a little tobacco, vermillion and beads. Gregg was willing to buy all his Mexican slaves and take them back to Chihuahua, but only a boy took the opportunity to return to his Mexican family.

8. Courlander. *The Fourth World of the Hopis*, 185-90.

9. *Report of Explorations For A Railroad Route, Near The Thirty-Fifth Parallel Of North Latitude, From The Mississippi River To The Pacific Ocean*: By Lieutenant A. W. Whipple, Corps Of Topographical Engineers, Assisted By Lieutenant J. C. Ives, Corps Of Topographical Engineers, Vol. III, I., p. 129 of *Reports of-Explorations and Surveys To Ascertain the Most Practical and Economic Route For A Railroad From the Mississippi River To The Pacific Ocean, 1853-4*, 33d Congress, 2 d. Session, Senate Ex. Doc. No. 78, #760, (Washington: Beverly Tucker Printer, 1856); Grant Foreman, ed., *A Pathfinder in the Southwest: The Itinerary of Lieutenant A.W. Whipple During His Explorations for a Railroad Route from Fort Smith to Los Angeles in the Year 1853 and 1854* (Norman: University of Oklahoma Press, 1941), 27, 57,148.

10. Foreman, *Whipple, Railroad Explorations of 1853 and 1854*, 259-60.

11. Foreman, Whipple, *Railroad Exploration of 1853-54*, 260.

12. Lyman, *The Overland Journey from Utah to California*, 188-92.

13. *Ibid*, 188-89;for an excellent study of Mojave Desert Indian problems of the 1860s, read Dennis Casebier's *The Battle of Camp Cady* (1972) and *Carleton's Pah-Ute Campaign* (1972); Walker, *Back Door to California,* 212-18.

14. Lyman, *The Overland Journey from Utah to California*, 189-91; Walker, *Back Door to California*, 212-18.

15. Brandon, *Book of Indians,* 352-53.

16. Jones, *The Trial of Don Pedro León Luján,* 32.

17. LeRoy R. Hafen and Ann W. Hafen, eds., *The Diaries of William Henry Jackson, Frontier Photographer to California and Return, 1866-67; and with the Hayden Surveys to the Central Rockies, 1873, and to the Utes and Cliff Dwellers, 1874, from the Far West and the Rockies Historical Series 1820-1875* (Glendale: The Arthur H. Clark Company, 1959), X, 121.

18. Vicente P Gómez, *"Venta de ninos indios en los Angeles" in Lo Que Sabe Cosas de California,* microfilm, California Archives C-D , 85-86, Los Angeles County Museum, original in Bancroft library, Berkeley. Gomez was once secretary for Governor Micheltorena, and later clerk for Bancroft. When he wrote his memoirs in 1876 he seemed sharp.

Chapter 10

Effects Never Ending

1. McNitt, *The Indian Slave Trader*, 341-42; Palmer, *Pahute Indian Legends*, ix.

2. Palmer, *Pahute Indian Legends*, ix.

3. Joseph H.Toulouse, Jr., "Navajo Slave Blanket," *Desert Magazine*, February 1929, 22-23.

4. A. L. Kroeber "Olive Oatman Return"; A. L. Kroeber, and Clifton B. Kroeber, "Olive Oatman's First Account of Her Captivity Among the Mohave"; Rasmussen, "Tale of Kindness Didn't Fit Notion of Savage Indian." Dillon, "Tragedy at Oatman Flat: Massacre, Captivity, Mystery";Galvin, "Cloudwoman: The Life of Olive Oatman, An Old `California Indian Captive."

5.Kane, "A View from Ridge Route," 169-70.

6.Charles Wood, Chemehuevi Chairman, MMS., "Convocation of 14th Annual Old Spanish Trail Conference," Barstow, June 8, 2007; Walker, *Back Door to California*, 30.

7. A.L. Kroeber, *Handbook of American Indians*, 614-15, 883.

8. Donna Yocum, Personal Interview. Portland, October 21, 2008 and Barstow, May 9, 2007. *Repatriation Ceremony March 11, 2006.* Seven Feathers Corporation/San Fernando Band of Mission Indians, 2006. This moving ceremony captures the emotions of modern, formerly considered extinct Vanyume and Kitanamuk Indians of the Mojave Desert, reburying their dead in the western Mojave Desert. Two of these remains had DNA that matched Donna Yucum, Vice Chairwoman of the San Fernando Band of Mission Indians. This exciting news proves that the Vanyume of the Mojave Desert are not extinct.

Yocum is a Vanyume Indian who descended from Mission captives taken from the Mojave Desert in the 1830s; John Valen-zuela, Personal interview, Barstow, May 9, 2007, December 22, 2008, telephone conversation, December 17, 2008. Valenzu-ela is a Vanyume Indian, descended from Indian taken to the San Fernando Mission. He is Chairman of San Fernando Band of Mission Indians and Donna Yocum is Vice Chairwoman; Judy O'Rourke, "DNA Links Ancient, Modern Indians," Santa Clarita: *The Signal,* 2005. *http://www.scvhistory.com/scvhistory/sg052205-indians.htm.*

9.   Clifford J. Walker, "Timbisha Shoshone Tribe," MMS for Mojave River Valley Museum, 2002. The Timbisha has control over 300 acres at Furnace Creek, over 3,000 acres elsewhere, in-cluding Lido Ranch in Nevada Said tribal member Barbara Dur-ham: "We believe the land and water are really ours. It is the tribe's wish to protect this area particularly. The tribe will help preserve these sites."

10.   Laird, *The Chemehuevis,* 168-82.

11.   Walker, "Los Coyotes Indians and the Mojave Desert," MMS, Barstow, 2006.

12.   Patricia Kuhlhoff, telephone conversersation Santa Fe, September 18, 2008.

13.   *Los Angeles Plaza Church Death Records,* translated through the courtesy of William Mason, Los Angeles County Museum.

GLOSSARY

Alcalde—in New Mexico sometimes the word "alcalde-mayor" was used. It comes from Arabic meaning village chief; a native appointed or elected to be in charge of village or district, sometimes with great authority to make or pass laws, enforce the laws and judge whether a person is guilty of violated the same law. When the Americans took over Mexican territory, sometime they continued using the alcalde; mining districts often elected an alcalde in charge of a mining camp.

Almudes—dry or liquid measure about 6.87 quartz or 5.133 liters. Spanish and Mexican measurements were slightly different.

Atole—Finely ground corn meal, made into a refreshing drink or mush. Used as trail food, such as along the Old Spanish Trail.

Ayuntamiento—City council government, usually for a large district. The *Ayuntamiento* of Los Angeles covered the whole Los Angeles basin.

Bando—Law or proclamation announced by the governor of New Mexico for example.

Binaalté—Navajo word meaning slave belonging to the Navajo.

Cacique—Spanish word from Haiti meaning "lord," "prince"—a native chief.

Californios—Plural for the Mexicans who lived in California before the Americans took over California in 1848. These people like American colonists in the 18th century thought themselves different from the "Mother Country" people. These Californios were special people, not just Mexicans in California.

Chaguanosos—coined by a California governor to encompass travelers who came from New Mexico across the Old Spanish Trail in the 1830s who were French-Canadian trappers, American trappers, New Mexicans, Utes and Hudson Bay (British) trappers. The derogatory term meant "Thieves of Many Nations" because they stole horses and mules from up and down the state.

Chemehuevi—A dialect of the Southern Paiue, a Numic branch of he Uto-Aztecan language. These Indians lived in the eastern Mojave Desert in the historic times expanded to both sides of the Colorado River below the Mojave Indians and by Bill Williams Fork in the Chemehuevi Valley. These were often called Paiute. They call themselves *Niwiwi*: meaning the People.

Cimarrones—Runaway mission Indians, *neophyte* refugees.

Colorado Desert—Desert of Riverside and Imperial counties.

Encomienda—Spanish system whereby the one who receives a land grant has custody of the Indians on that land grant. He must take care of the needs of the Indians, mainly the spiritual and educational needs to allow the Indians to become Spanish citizens. Indians were generally allowed to hunt or fish to survive on the land if that was appropriate. *Encomenderos* are those who are granted land with responsibilities of the Indians or were granted "free" Indians in contract to work. See Gibson's *Spain in America* for a brief history of *encomienda* and *encomenderos*.

Fanega—dry measure of about 1 ½ bushels.

Forks of the Road—(Forks in the Road)—The camping spot at this point the road forks to Las Vegas and to Fort Mojave on the Colorado River of Indians, New Mexicans, and trappers on the Mojave River just east of Minneola Road in Yermo. The Mexicans called it *Punta de Agua* (Point of Water) because the Manix fault forces the water to the surface.

Genízaros—New Mexican and Spanish term for a "wild" Indians who have accepted the Spanish or Mexican culture (society), religion and who have lost or given up their Native American identity. Some were given pueblos and land and were quite often place in buffer locations to protect larger settlement. *Genízaros* inhabited Abiquiu and Taos and they formed a militia that could be called on to protect the frontier or make punitive raids on warlike Indians. The pueblo of Saint Thomas Apostle of Abiquiu had a settlement of *genízaros*. Likewise were towns like San Miguel del Vado, Belen and Taos.

Gente de razon—Civilized Spanish, Mexican or mestizos, sons or daughters of mixed Spanish and Indians.

Kitanemuk—Takic speakers of Uto-Aztecan Language group, closely related to Serrano and Vanyume Indians, sometimes called Kitanemuk-Serrano, sometimes identifies with Ft. Tejon Indians. Now descendents are joint members of part of the San Fernando Band of Mission Indians who are seeking recognition by the Federal government.

League—Spanish measurement of approximately three miles.

Mayordomo—the boss, or the field leader of a rancho or mission in New Mexico or California.

Mestizos—offspring of European and Indian relationship.

Neophytes—a newly converted Indian to Catholicism, often used by the Spanish to help colonize new areas or to help convert new souls to the Church.

Old Spanish Trail—The mule caravan trail from New Mexico to Los Angeles. Since it was started by New Mexicans in 1829-30, it was neither old nor Spanish. Fremont commented in 1844 that this would lead to the Spanish Trail; hence we have a name that stuck.

Paiute—Piede, Pied, Pahute, Pah ute, Piute *Pah* means water; therefore these are "Water Utes." They speak a Numic Branch of the Uto-Aztecan language. In the Southern Paiutes who migrated back into California were called Chemehuevi. The Paiutes in the Owens Valley are called Northern Paiutes, some migrating into northern California and into Oregon, becoming the Bannock. Generally American travelers in the 19th century called these desert Indians Paiute. Derogatorily, they were called "Diggers."

Peon, peonage system—A New Mexican servant system whereby sometimes the servant never escapes his or her obligations to the rancho or church—almost like the old song "another day older, another day deeper in debt-- I owe my soul to the company store." Debts tied the worker to his "owner" and these peons sometimes never worked off their debts. The system was outlawed in 1867. but still continued.

Piñole—Parched or roasted corn meal, finely ground and mixed with water. It is very nourishing and refreshing trail food used along the Old Spanish Trail. It may be mixed with cinnamon or brown sugar. Indian piñole is made from ground wild seed.

Prefect—District judge used both in California and New Mexico. *Prefect* is also like a Mexican county jurisdiction. For awhile there wer two Prefects in southern California, one at Santa Barbara and the other at San Diego.

Provincias Internas—A new province made up in the 1770s of Sonora, New Mexico, California to help better control this vast frontier area of New Spain.

Repartimiento--"to have, to hold, and to possess." King of Spain authorized conquistadors to partial (grant) land to soldiers or friends in the 1500s.

Santa Fe Trail—The wagon freighting road from Missouri to Taos and Santa Fe during the 1820s. It had two branches, one called the Cimarron Cut Off. The Mexican authorities allowed trading between the United States and Mexican territories, whereas the Spanish government did not permit trade. When Mexico took over New Mexico, Missouri freighters and businessmen were quick to take advantage of the new opportunities.

Tirutas—Spanish word for New Mexican heavy weave blankets, made from "wild sheep" wool, traded to Californians, usually used for horse blankets. Mojave Indians and New Mexican traders brought these to Los Angeles over the Old Spanish Trail and the Mojave Indian Trail.

Ute—Also Yuta, Utah, horse Ute, A Numic speaking Uto-Aztecan language migrated from desert about 1000 years ago. Some obtain the horse and even became Plains Indians, raiding weaker Ute (non-horse Utes) and Paiutes. They generally occupied the Colorado Plateau, eastern half of Utah and most of Colorado into northern New Mexico. Abiquiu was their ancestral land in New Mexico.

Vanyume—Desert Serrano or Takic branch of Uto-Aztecan language speakers who lived around the Mojave River and in the mountains to the west and in western Antelope Valley. They were thought to be extinct, but this book shows they are alive and well.

Wickiup—small, light structures used by hunter-gatherers, usually in the desert a brush shelter, but may be conical shaped, domed and even lean-tos and windbreaks.

WORKS CITED

GOVERNMENT SOURCES:

Cuch,Forrest S. *A History of Utah's American Indians.* Salt Lake City: Utah State Department of Indian Affairs, 2003.

Garfielde, S. and F. A. Snyder, eds. *Compiled Laws of the State of California, Containing All the Acts of the Legislature of a Public and General Nature, Now in Force, Passed at the Sessions of 1850-51-52-53, To Which Are Prefixed the Declaration of Independence, The Constitution of the United States and of California, the Treaty of Queretaro, and the Nationalization Laws of the United States.* Boston: Franklin Printing House, 1853.

Brevet Col. J. C. Fremont, *The Exploring Expeditions to the Rocky Mountains in the Year 1842 and to Oregon and Northern California in Year 1843-44.* In *Public Documents,* by Order of the Senate of the U.S., 2nd Session of the 28 Congress XI (Washington: 1845).

Los Angeles Plaza Church Death Records, translated through the courtesy of William Mason, Los Angeles County Museum.

Minute Book of the Illustrious Ayuntamiento, II, session of February 11, 1837, MSS. OfficialTranslation in the Los Angeles City Clerk's Office.

Minute Book of the Illustrious Ayuntamiento Census of 1836 and 1844, III, MSS. Official Translation in the Los Angeles City Clerk's Office.

Muscupiabe (No. 75) Transcript of proceeding before U.S. Land Commission. Michael White. Document 79, Beattie Collection, Huntington Library.

Underhill, Ruth. The*Northern Paiute Indians in California and Nevad*a. Branch of Indian Affairs, Bureau of Indian Affairs, 1941, 55. Washburn, Wilcomb E. *The American Indian and the UnitedStates: A Documentary History,* Vol. I, *Smithsonian* Institute. New York: Random House, 1973.

Whipple, A. W., "Itinerary," 84, in *Report of Explorations for a Railway Route, Near the Thirty-fifth Parallel of North Latitude...,*Vol. 3 of Pacific Survey Reports, 33 Cong., 2 Sess., Sen. Ex. Doc. 78.

DIARIES, JOURNALS:

Bell, Major Horace. *Reminiscences of a Ranger or Early Times in Southern California*. Santa Barbara: Wallace Hebberd, 1927.

Coues, Elliot. *On the Trail of a Spanish Pioneer, the Diary and itinerary of Francisco Garces (Missionary Priest) in his travels through Sonora, Arizona, and California, 1775-1776. Translated from an Official Contemporaneous Copy of the Original Spanish Manuscript, and Edited with Copious Notes in Two Volumes*. New York: Francis P. Harper, 1900, I.

Caughey, John Walton, ed. *The Indians of Southern California in 1852: The B. D. Wilson Report and a Selection of Contemporary Comment*. San Marino: Huntington Library, 1952.

Dakin, Susanna Bryant. *A Scotch Paisano: Hugo Reid's Life in California, 1832-1851, Derived from His Correspondence*. Berkeley: University of California Press, 1939. For Wilson's complete memoirs see Robert Glass Cleland, *Pathfinders*. Los Angeles: Powell Publishing Company, 1929.

Dale, Harrison C., ed. *The Ashley-Smith Exploration and Discovery of the Central Route to the Pacific, 1822-1829*. Cleveland: The Arthur H. Clark Company, 1918.

Esparza, Juan Bautista.*Vida California, 1834-47*. MS California Archives C D, 44. Microfilm at Los Angeles County Museum, original in Bancroft Library, Berkeley.

Farnham, Thomas J. *Adventures in California with Travels in Oregon*. Pictorial Edition. New York: No publisher listed in rebound copy at University of Southern California Library, 1849.

Foreman, Grant, ed. *A Pathfinder in the Southwest: The Itinerary of Lieutenant A. W. Whipple during his explorations for a railway route from Fort Smith to Los Angeles in the years 1853 and 1854*. Norman: University of Oklahoma Press, 1941. See also Whipple, 127, for another example of Mexican slavery in Central New Mexico.

Foy, Mary E., ed. "By Ox Team from Salt Lake to Los Angeles, 1850: A Memoir by David W. Chessman." *The Historical Society of Southern California Annual Publication*, XIV (1930).

Fremont, John Charles. *Memoirs of My Life*. Chicago: Belford, Clarke & Company, 1887, I._____. *The Exploring Expeditions to the*

Rocky Mountains, Oregon and California. Buffalo: Geo. Derby & Co.Publishers, 1849.

Gomez, Vincente P. *"Venta de ninos indios en Los Angeles,"* in *Lo Que Sabe Sobre Cosas de California.* Microfilm, California Archives C-D. Los Angeles County Museum, original in Bancroft Library.

Gordon, Mary McD., ed. *Through Indian Country to California: John P. Sherburne's Diary of the Whipple Expedition 1853-54.* Stanford, CA: Stanford University Press, 1988.

Gregg, Josiah. *The Commerce of the Prairies by Josiah Gregg,* edited by Milo Milton Quaife. Lincoln: University of Nebraska Press, 1967.

Hafen, LeRoy R. and Ann W. Hafen, eds. *The Diaries of William Henry Jackson, Frontier Photographer to California and Return, 1866-67; and with the Hayden Surveys to the Central Rockies, 1873, and to the Utes and Cliff Dwellers, 1874,* in the *Far West and the Rockies Historical Series 1820-1875.* Vol. X. Glendale: The Arthur H. Clark Company, 1959.

Kroeber, A. L. and C. B. Kroeber. *A Mohave War Reminiscence 1854-1880.* New York: Dover Publication Inc., 1994.

Lorton, William B. *The Diaries of William B. Lorton: September 1848 - January 1850.* MSS, C-F 190 Bancroft Library, Berkeley, California.

Lugo, Don José Del Carmen. "Vida de un Rancho," dictated to Thomas Savage, 1877, translated by Helen Pruitt Beattie. *Quarterly of San Bernardino County Museum Association* (Winter, 1961).

Nuez, Fr. Joaquin Pasquel. *Diary of Fr. Joaquin Pasquel Nuez, Minister of San Gabriel and Chaplain of the Expedition Against the Mojave Indian, Begun by Lieutenant Gabriel Moraga, Novenber 1819.* Translated by George Beattie. Copy in Walker's *Back Door to California: The Story of the Mojave River Trail,* Appendix C. Also in Huntington Library.

Stratton, R. B. *Captivity of the Oatman Girls.* Salem: Oregon Teachers Monthly, 1909.

Thwaites, Reuben Gold, ed. *The Personal Narrative of James O. Pattie of Kentucky.* Cleveland: The Arthur H. Clark Company, 1905.

Van Winkle, F. A. "The Foremothers Tell of Olden Times," *Gold Rush Stories of Women Pioneers.* San Francisco Museum. *http://www.sf-museum.net/hist5/foremoms.html*

BOOKS:

Ames, Kenneth M. "Slavery, Household Production, and Demography on the Southern Northwest Coast: Cables, Tacking, and Rope walks," in Catherine M. Cameron, editor, *Invisible Citizens: Captives and their Consequences.*(Salt Lake City: The University of Utah Press, 2008.

Blue, Martha. *Indian Trader: The Life and Times of J. L. Hubbell.* Walnut, CA.: Kiva Publishing, 2000.

Bailey, Paul. *Walkara, Hawk of the Mountains.* Los Angeles: Westernlore Press, 1954.

Bancroft, H.H. *The History of California 1801-1824,* II. Santa Barbara: Wallace Hebberd, 1966.

_____. *The History of California.* San Francisco: The History Company, 1884, III.

_____. *The History of California 1840-1845,* IV. Santa Barbara: Wallace Hebberd, 1969.

Beattie, George William and Helen Pruitt Beattie. *Heritage of the Valley, San Bernardino's First Century.* Pasadena: San Pasqual Press, 1939.

Beck, Warren. A.*New Mexico: A History of Four Centuries.* Norman: University of Oklahoma Press, 1926.

Blackmar, Frank W. *Spanish Institutions of the Southwest.* Glorieta: The Rio Grande Press, Inc., 1976.

Blackhawk, Ned. *Violence over the Land: Indians and Empires in the Early American West.* Cambridge: Harvard University Press, 2006.

Bonner, D., ed. *The Life and Adventures of James P. Beckwourth.* New York: Alfred A. Knoph, 1931.

Brewer, William H. *Up and Down California 1860-1864.* editor Francis P. Farquhar. Berkeley: University of California Press, 1966.

Brooks, James F. "Captive, Concubine, Servant, Kin: A Historian Divines Experience in Archaeological Slaveries,"in Catherine M. Cameron, editor. *Invisible Citizens: Captives and their Consequences.* Salt Lake City: The University of Utah Press, 2008.

Brandon, William. *The American Handbook of Indians.* New York: Dell Publishing Co., 1964.

Brooks, James F. *Captives & Cousins & Slavery: Kinship, and Community in the Southwest Borderlands.* Chapel Hill: University of North

Carolina Press, 2002.

Brown, John, Jr. and James Boyd, *History of San Bernardino and Riverside Counties*. Chicago: Western Historical Association, 1922, I.

Burrill, Richard. *River of Sorrows: Life History of the Maidu-Nisenan Indians*. Happy Camp, CA: Naturegraph Publisher, Inc., 1988.

Chapman, Charles E. *A History of California: The Spanish Period*. New York: The Macmillan Company, 1936.

Cook, Sherburne. "Franciscan Missionaries," nd, publisher unknown, 26-27, copy in possession of author. This list is the 1797 reason given by 30 Indians for running away from the mission in San Francisco.

Courlander, Harold. *The Fourth World of the Hopis: The Epic Story of the Hopi Indians as Preserved in their Legends and Traditions*. Albuquerque: University of New Mexico Press, 1971.

Crum, Sally. *People of the Red Earth: American Indians of Colorado*. Santa Fe: Ancient City Press, 1996.

DeBoer, Warren R. "Wrenched Bodies," in Catherine M. Cameron, editor. *Invisible Citizens: Captives and their Consequences*. Salt Lake City: The University of Utah Press, 2008.

Drucker, Philip. *Indians of the Northwest Coast*. Garden City: The Natural History Press, 1963.

Engelhardt. Fray Zephyrin. *San Gabriel Mission and the Beginnings of Los Angeles*. San Gabriel, 1927.

_____. *The Missions and Missionaries of California*. San Francisco: James H. Berry Co., 1913.

Jack Forbes, *Native Americans of California and Nevada* Happy Camp, CA: Naturegraph, 2006.

Frank, L. and Kim Hogeland. *First Families: A Photographic History of California Indians*. Berkeley: Heyday Books, 2007.

Gibson, Charles. *Spain in America*. New York: Harper Torchbooks, 1966

Gottfredson, _____. *History of Indian Depredations in Utah*. nd.np.

Jones, Oakah L., Jr. *Los Paisinos: Spanish Settlers on the Northern Frontiers of New Spain*. Norman: University of Oklahoma Press, 1979.

Jones, Sondra. *The Trial of Don Pedro León Luján: The Attack Against Indian Slavery and Mexican Trade in Utah*. Salt Lake City: University of Utah Press, 1949.

Kane, Bonnie Ketterl. "A View from Ridge Route," Vol. 1 of *the First People*. Frazier Park, CA: Bonnie's Books, 2001.

Kroeber, A.L. *Handbook of Indians of California.* New York: Dover Publications, Inc., 1976.

Kroeber, A.L. "Yurok Law and Custom," in *The California Indians, A Source Book,* edited by R.F. Heizer and M.A. Whipple. Berkeley: University of California Press, 1971.

Laird, Carobeth. *The Chemehuevis.* Banning: Malki Press, 1976.

Lyman, Edward Leo. *The Overland Journey from Utah to California: Wagon Travel from the City of the Saints to the City of the Angels.* Reno: University of Nevada Press, 2004.

Martin, Debra L. "Ripped Flesh and Torn Souls: Skeletal Evidence for Captivity and Slavery from the La Plata Valley, New Mexico, AD 1100-1300," in Catherine M. Cameron, editor. *Invisible Citizens: Captives and their Consequences.* Salt Lake City: The University of Utah Press, 2008.

McNitt. Frank. *The Indian Trader.* Norman: University of Oklahoma Press, 1962.

Menchaca, Martha. *Recovering History Constructing Race: The Indians, Black and White--Roots of Mexican Americans.* Austin: University of Texas, 2001.

Morgan, Dale L. *Jedehiah Smith and the Opening of the West.* Lincoln: University of Nebraska Press, 1964.

Niethammer, Carolyn. *Daughters of the Earth: The Lives and Legends of American Indian Women.* The Website of Simon and Schuster, Inc. 1955. http://www.simonsays.com/content/cfm?tab=1&pid=407274

Palmer, William R. *Pahute Indian Legends.* Salt Lake City: Deseret Books Company Publishers, 1946.

Sanchez, Joseph P. *Explorers, Traders, and Slavers: Forging the Old Spanish Trail.* Salt Lake City: University of Utah Press, 1997.

Saunders, Charles Francis and J. Smeaton Chase. *The California Padres and Their Missions.* Boston: Houghton Mifflin Company, 1915.

Secrest, William B. *When the Great Spirit Died: The Destruction of the California Indians 1850-1860.* Sanger, CA: World Dancer Press, 2003.

Sheridan, Thomas E. and Nancy J. Parezo, editors. *Paths of Life: American Indians of the Southwest and Northern Mexico.* Tucson: The University of Arizona Press, 1996.

Sullivan, Maurice S. *The Travels of Jedediah Smith.* Santa Ana: The Fine Arts Press, 1934.

Sunseri, Alvin R. *Seeds of Discord: New Mexico in the Aftermanth of the American Conquest, 1846-1861*. Chicago: Nelson-Hall 1979.

Trafzer, Clifford E. and Joel R. Hyer, editors. *"Exterminate Them"—Written Accounts of the Murder, Rape, and Enslavement of Native Americans during the California Gold Rush, 1848-1868*. East Lansing: Michigan State University Press, 1999.

Walker, Clifford J. *Back Door to California: The Story of the Mojave River Trail*. Barstow: Mojave River Valley Museum, 1986.

Waters, Frank. *Masked Gods: Navaho and Pueblo Ceremonialism*. New York: Ballentine Books, 1973.

_____.*Book of the Hopi*. New York: The Viking Press, 1961.

MANUSCRIPTS:

Head, Lafayette. "Statement of Mr. Head of Abiqui[u] in regard to buying and selling of Pah-ute Indian Children April 30, 1852." RI 2150.San Marino: Huntington Library.

Jorgensen, John L. "Spanish Traders and American Trappers," from *A History of Castle Valley to 1890*. A masters thesis, 1955, from Emery County Archives. Castle Dale, Utah.

Mia, Marie Martinez." Prayer." *Repatriation Ceremony*, Mojave Desert: March 11, 2006. MMS in possession of author.

Real-Galvez, Estevan. *Identifying Captivity and Capturing Indentity: Narratives of American Indians Slavery in New Mexico and Colorado, 1776-1934*. A dissertation. University of Michigan, 2002.

Valenzuela, John. "All Those that Wonder Are Not Lost!" Hesperia: 2009. MMS in possession of author.

Walker, Clifford J. "Los Coyotes Indians and the Mojave Desert," MMS, Barstow: 2006.

_____. "Timbisha Shoshone Tribe." MMS for Mojave River Valley Museum, 2002.

Wood, Charles. "Convocation of 14th Annual Old Spanish Trail Conference." Barstow, June 8, 2007. MMS in possession of author.

Yocum, Donna Smith. "Words to My Ancestors," *Repatriation Ceremony*. Mojave Desert: March11, 2006. MMS in possession of author

_____.. "You Did Not Become No More." Talk at *Repatriation Ceremony*. Mojave Desert, 2006. MMS in possession of author.

PERIODICALS:

Creer, Leland Hargrave. "Spanish—American Slave Trade in the Great Basin, 1800-1853." *New Mexico Historical Review* Vol. XXXIV, No. 3, July 1949.

Earle, David D. "The Mojave River and the Central Mojave Desert: Native Settlement, Travel, and Exchange in the Eighteenth and Nineteenth Centuries." *Journal of California and Great Basin Anthropology,* Vol I, No. 1. Banning: Malki Museum, Inc., 2005.

Dillon, Richard. "Tragedy at Oatman Flat: Massacre, Captivity, Mystery." *The American West,* March/April, 1981.

Galvin, Lynn. "Cloudwoman: The Life of Olive Oatman, An Old California Indian Captive." *The Californians,* Volume 13, No. 2. nd.

Galbaith [unknown]. "Turbulent Taos." Denver: The Press of the Territories, Number 18, 1970. This is Number 18 of a *Series of Western Americana.*

Heizer, Robert. "Impact of Colonization on the Native Californian Societies." *The Journal of San Diego History,* Winter 1878, Vol. 24, No. 1. *http:www.sandiegohistory.org/journal/78/impact.htm.*

Hill, Joseph J. "Ewing Young in the Fur Trade of the Far Southwest, 1822-1834," reprint from *Oregon Historical Quarterly,* XXIV, No. 1. Eugene: Koke-Tiffnay Co., 1923.

Kroeber, A. L. "Olive Oatman Return." *Anthropological Society Papers,* No. 4, Berkeley: 1950.

Lonnberg, Allan. "The Digger Indian Stereotype in California." *Journal of California and Great Basin Anthropology*, Vol. 3, No. 2, 1981.

O'Rourke, Judy. "DNA Links Ancient, Modern Indians." *Signal.* Santa Clarita Valley Historical Society, May 22, 2005.

Stockton, James D. *Spanish Trailblazers in the South San Joaquin 1772-1781.* Bakersfield: Kern County Historical Society, 1957.

Toulouse, Joseph H. Jr. "Navajo Slave Blanket." *Desert Magazine,* February 1929.

NEWSPAPERS:

Daily Alta California (San Francisco). April 7, 1855, October 21, 1861.

Daily Morning Call (San Francisco). November 24, December 10, 1858.

Rasmussen, Cecilia. "Tale of Kindness Didn't Fit Notion of Savage Indian." *Los Angeles Times,* July 16, 2000.

Sacramento Daily Union. July 31, October 1, 1860.

INTERVIEWS:

Adams, Rick. Personal Interview, Roseville, CA, September 19, 2008. Maidu Indian, at Maidu Interpretive Center, Roseville.

Earle, David. Personal Interview, Barstow, January 2007.

Kuhlhoff, Patricia. Telephone conversation, September 28, December 31, 2008.

Valenzuela, John. Personal Interview, Barstow, May 9, 2007, December 22, 2008, telephone interview December 17, 30, 2008.

Yocum, Donna. Personal Interview, Barstow, May 9, 2007 and Portland, Oregon, October 11, 2008. Telephone conversation, February 17, 2009.

MISCELLANEOUS

Chronology of Compulsory Indian Labor Laws in New Spain, Mexico, and the United States. Appendix C of unknown book, unknown author, in possession of author.

Geiger, Rev. Maynard. "Rev. Maynard Geiger, G.F.M., Supports Mis sions," no date or source, typed copy in possession of author. *"Genízaro"* in *New Mexico Historic Review,* volume unknown, 70, includes the definitions and history of the word, in posses sion of the author.

Repatriation Ceremony. March11, 2006, CD, San Fernando Band of Mission Indians. Seven Feathers Corporation/San Fernando Band of Mission Indians, 2006. This moving ceremony captures the emotions of modern, formerly considered extinct Vanyume and Kitanamuk Indians of the Mojave Desert, reburying their dead in the western Mojave Desert. Two of these remains had DNA that matched Donna Yucum, Vice Chairwoman of the San Fernando Band of Mission Indians. This exciting find proves that the Vanyume of the Mojave Desert are not extinct.

INDEX

A

B

C

Kroeber, A. L. · 87, 88, 95, 96, 117, 118, 119, 132

L

Lattimer · 76
Lonnberg, Allan · 9, 114, 128
Lorton, William · 10, 61, 62, 125
Los Angeles Selling Slaves · 58, 67, 68, 84, 130, 131, 133, 134, 138, 139
Los Angeles Plaza Church · 63, 93, 101, 126, 133
Lucero · 41
Lujan, Pedro Leon · 78
Lyman, Leo · 3, 44, 62, 122, 131

M

Maidu · 28, 69, 127
Maidu Walk · 69
Manypenny, Commissioner George W. · 74
Manzano Mountains · 86, 94
Marcy, Sec. of War · 61
Maria de la Luz · 63, 93, 101
Martin · 41
Martinez, Fray Luis Antonio · 31, 103, 105, 106
Mestas · 39
Mexicans · 1, 2, 3, 9, 11, 13, 15
Mia, Marie · 89, 97, 102, 103, 105, 106
Mission San Jose · 51, 57
Miwok Indians · 69
Mix, Commissioner Charles E. · 74
Moapa Reservation · 74
Modocs · 8
Mojave Desert · 2, 3, 4, 8, 15, 16, 17, 26, 50, 54, 57, 62, 82, 88, 93, 96, 101, 102, 103, 105, 128, 131, 132, 133, 134
Mojave River · 3, 4, 8, 16, 17, 26, 31, 32, 33, 38, 54, 57, 61, 62, 63, 82, 83, 84, 101, 108, 120, 123, 133, 137, 139
Mojave River Trail. · 31, 61, 83
Mollhausen, artist · 15, 33, 35, 75
Montesquieu · 40
Moraga, Lt. Gabriel · 31, 32, 120
Mormon Road · 3
Mormons · 44, 45, 46
Mory · 40, 41
Muscupiabit · 88, 96

N

Napa Valley · 71
Navajo · 7, 14, 39, 41, 46, 81, 84, 86, 87, 92, 94, 95, 100, 111, 132, 134
Navajos · 7, 13, 14, 23, 42, 46, 54, 75, 81, 84, 86, 94, 111
Negroes, freed · 70, 111
Nelson, Dadeane, Elder · 92, 100
New Mexican muleteers · 1

T

U

V

Valenzuela, John, Chair · 89, 97, 101, 102, 103, 104, 132, 133
Vallejo, Mariana · 69
Van Winkle, F. A. · 71, 128
Vanyume · 32, 33, 63, 88, 89, 96, 97, 101, 102, 103, 104, 105, 106, 132, 133, 137, 139
Vanyume tribe · 88, 96
Vargas, Don Diego de · 11, 12, 14
Vigil Francisco · 40, 55
Vineyard, Col. James R., Agent · 73

W

Wakara · 44, 45, 61, 62, 125
Walla Walla · 7, 28
Walpi · 12
War Against Gila Monster · 89, 97
Warner Ranch · 89, 97
Warren, Elizabeth Von Till· 38, 62, 77, 114, 120 121, 123, 128 129, 130
Wessels, Capt. H. W. · 75
Whipple, Lt. A. · 16, 23, 75, 81, 82, 117, 118, 119, 129, 130, 131
White, Michael ·, Miguel Blanco,.. 64, 65, 66, 69, 118, 126
Wichcaya · finding stolen wife..14, 15
Wilburn, Robert · 82
Wild horses · 27
Williams, Isaac · 16, 61, 62, 82, 83, 125, 137
Williams, Rev. Joseph · 54
Wilson, Ben · 57, 58, 59, 65, 124, 126
Wood, Charles, Chemehuevi Chair · 63, 68, 88, 96, 126, 127, 128, 129, 132
Wootton, Uncle, trapper · 41, 42
Work, John · 30, 51, 69
Workman, William · 65

Y

Yainax. · 30
Yavapai · 18, 23
Yocum, Donna · 88, 89, 96, 97, 101, 102, 103, 104, 105, 106, 132, 133
Young, Clara 45
Young, Gov. Brigham · 53, 78, 79, 84, 88, 96, 111, 123
Young, Sally 45
Yount, George C. · 71
Yuma · 16, 17, 21, 22, 87, 95, 118
Yurok · 7, 28, 119

Z

Zía Pueblo · 11